YOUR FIELD GUIDE TO MAKING BETTER DECISIONS

OUTSMARTING
V.U.C.A.

YOUR FIELD GUIDE TO MAKING BETTER DECISIONS

OUTSMARTING V.U.C.A.

ACHIEVING SUCCESS in a
Volatile, **U**ncertain, **C**omplex, &
Ambiguous World

DON GILMAN, Ed.D.

Published by Advantage, Charleston, South Carolina.
Member of Advantage Media Group.

ADVANTAGE is a registered trademark, and the Advantage colophon is a trademark of Advantage Media Group, Inc.

Printed in the United States of America.

ISBN: 978-1-59932-620-7
LCCN: 2016953409

Cover design by Katie Biondo.

This publication is designed to provide accurate and authoritative information in regard to the subject matter covered. It is sold with the understanding that the publisher is not engaged in rendering legal, accounting, or other professional services. If legal advice or other expert assistance is required, the services of a competent professional person should be sought.

 Advantage Media Group is proud to be a part of the Tree Neutral® program. Tree Neutral offsets the number of trees consumed in the production and printing of this book by taking proactive steps such as planting trees in direct proportion to the number of trees used to print books. To learn more about Tree Neutral, please visit **www.treeneutral.com.**

Advantage Media Group is a publisher of business, self-improvement, and professional development books. We help entrepreneurs, business leaders, and professionals share their Stories, Passion, and Knowledge to help others Learn & Grow. Do you have a manuscript or book idea that you would like us to consider for publishing? Please visit **advantagefamily.com** or call **1.866.775.1696.**

TABLE OF CONTENTS

INTRODUCTION

W hat decisions have you made that, in hindsight, have proved to be either significantly or completely wrong? Maybe the decisions were simply mistakes, or perhaps they just did not lead to the result that you thought they would. Have you ever wished for a do-over?

If you were to go through a diagnostic process—a fault tree analysis, an Ishikawa diagram, or a fishbone—what would you find was the root cause? Was it the personalities of the people involved? Was it that not enough time was spent gathering information or data (or gathering the wrong data)? Was it that the leader made the decision and no one on the team said anything even though they knew it was not the best decision? What would you do differently the next time?

Perhaps the situation ended up being more unexpected or unstable than you thought (**Volatility**). Perhaps you were missing some key information (**Uncertainty**). Perhaps the situation had many interconnected parts or pieces and the volume of data was simply overwhelming (**C**omplexity). Or perhaps the situation was full of unknowns, and any causal relationships were completely unclear (**A**mbiguity). Congratulations! You have just experienced some of the challenges in a VUCA environment!

And these challenges, and many more like them, are exactly why outsmarting VUCA matters.

Maybe you chose to buy a house that was beyond your means, believing that your income would go up or that you'd be able to cut enough corners to make it all work. Now, looking back, you realize that you didn't examine enough data, or you only looked at data that supported your decision, or you made assumptions based on gut feeling. Perhaps one look at the relevant data (or perhaps the lack of relevant data) would have called your decision into question. What information did you have that your salary was going to go up? What guarantees did you have that you'd be able to make cuts in other areas? (Did you really think your utilities would stay the same in a bigger house?)

The problem so many of us face is that we avoid those questions that make us uncomfortable. And we don't like thinking reflectively on where we made bad decisions. Yet that's exactly how we learn.

Paul "Bear" Bryant, longtime head coach of the University of Alabama football team, said, "When you make a mistake, there are only three things you should ever do about it: admit it, learn from it, and don't repeat it." The problem isn't only making a mistake. It's also repeating the same mistake over and over again.

In organizations, situations like these are critical. Say you made the decision to invest in the development of a new product. Why? Well, you believed that if you built it, they would come. But when the customers don't come, you're left trying to figure out what happened. It's tempting to blame external forces—the customers don't know a good thing when they see it, the economy is working against us, a competitor is doing something underhanded, or our marketing effort missed the mark. Most of us are actually quite skilled in making excuses. But if you peel back the layers of the problem, what do you find? Could it have been because you based your "market analysis" solely on a conversation with your cousin Sal? He thought it would be a really cool product, so you went for it. But in the end, Sal was your only customer.

Why didn't you pause to adequately assess the risks? What stopped you from looking for data to find what you didn't know? Did you completely overlook a blind spot? Did you rely on the ideas of a homogenous team, one where everyone thought the same way?

Whether you're an individual contributor, a manager, or the leader of a major corporation, the key to ending the pain of bad decisions is to start with where it hurts, figure out why it hurts, and then figure out how to avoid that pain in the future.

How do you do that? You get better at outsmarting VUCA, individually as well as in your team, your group, or your organization.

How do you outsmart VUCA? You actively challenge assumptions, expose blind spots, and leverage diverse perspectives in order to arrive at better decisions. You add in the "offramps," the checkpoints after you make a critical decision to reevaluate and ensure that your decision was the best one.

Outsmarting VUCA is an active process that needs to happen regularly in life and on the job. Every day, we need to make decisions, come to conclusions, or take some action; this is when outsmarting VUCA is most valuable . . . when the stakes are high.

IN THE WORKPLACE

Today's workplaces are filled with people who simply do not have the skills to outsmart VUCA. Many well-educated people did not receive the type of education in college that forced them to question their own assumptions and the assumptions of others, and they often don't possess the emotional intelligence to interact well with others—they're opinionated, convinced they are correct, and not even swayed by solid logic. For example, many workplaces are filled with subject-matter experts (SMEs) who feel their value is based on their knowledge, opinions, and experience. To admit they don't know everything, or to entertain the possibility that they may be wrong, challenges their status as a SME in their mind. The reality is that our SMEs should be the *most* open to challenges.

Unfortunately, in my twenty-five-plus years of working with a wide variety of highly technical companies, I have observed—almost without exception—a heavy reliance on subject-matter experts, and all too often SMEs, with the best of intentions, end up leading the organization down the primrose path to less-than-stellar decisions. That's not working in today's fast-moving VUCA environment—the thinking that worked yesterday, the thinking that established them as a SME, simply doesn't work as well today, and it almost certainly won't work well tomorrow.

Compounding this VUCA environment is the challenge in the workplace to bridge diversity gaps. People bring to the table a multitude of different perspectives. Unlike past decades, today we are exposed to a plethora of backgrounds, cultures, ages, and experiences in the workplace today—for example, many organizations have four different and distinct generations in their workplace and we do our best to tolerate each other. Diversity is not something just to be tolerated, it's something to be leveraged; the different ways of thinking that we have access to today are a huge asset when it comes to outsmarting VUCA, as you'll learn throughout this book.

Leaders of organizations especially need to understand how to outsmart VUCA. In truth, many leaders want their team members to challenge their (the leader's) assumptions, but they don't know how to communicate that message to their employees. They really don't want to be surrounded by "yes men." They know that, in order to make good decisions, they must have accurate and complete information.

But employees are often afraid to provide honest feedback out of fear that they will be punished for differing with the boss. So it's a quandary. How do you create an environment in which employees are respectful and follow the leader but that also allows controversial or conflicting evidence or opinions when employees feel the boss is making the wrong decision?

HOW DO I KNOW WHAT I KNOW?

I began my career in the aerospace industry after earning degrees in engineering physics and nuclear engineering. Working on the Titan IV missile program, I recognized that my effectiveness was significantly limited by my inability to influence others, including management. I went back to school, earning a master's degree in engineering management. Even that new knowledge was not enough to skillfully expose errors in thinking (both my own and others) in a non-career-limiting way. After switching to the automotive industry in the late 90s, living and working in Europe for a few years, and continuing to be frustrated by "inside-the-box" thinking, I again returned to school to earn my doctorate in organization change. This combination of deep technical knowledge and broad leadership and management experience provides a unique diversity of thought that offers numerous tools to outsmart VUCA.

For over twenty-five years, I have helped companies and individuals learn how to accurately assess their complex environment, recognize and challenge their own assumptions, make the best decisions possible, and take action to achieve success. As a seasoned consultant and coach to senior management, I understand the ins and outs of outsmarting VUCA and what it takes to develop into an individual or an organization that knows how to go through the process and come out with the best decision available.

I have had the good fortune of being able to fine-tune my methods in a global VUCA environment. One of my recent engagements with a Fortune 100 company involved a multi-year project to launch an expansion of a North American-based business into the European market. It involved introducing a new, ambiguous, emerging technology in the midst of a volatile economy while dealing with an uncertain cadre of competitors and a complex network of customers and suppliers. I discovered what worked . . . and what didn't!

FOR INDIVIDUALS, BUSINESSES

Through my experiences, I've developed highly efficient and effective processes for improving individual and team thinking to outsmart VUCA. These processes are explained in the chapters that follow. First, I'll outline some of the common errors we see in thinking every day, and then I'll outline ways to identify faulty arguments, both in ourselves and in others. There is also a chapter that explains how the VUCA process works for individuals; those processes carry over into the succeeding chapter, which addresses how the process works in groups.

As an individual, the process for outsmarting VUCA allows you to methodically and deliberately explore a problem from multiple angles and perspectives in order to arrive at the best decision possible.

In the workplace, the process for outsmarting VUCA allows for employees to have a voice, even if that voice expresses a differing idea or conclusion. It creates an environment in which the leader has a greater likelihood of getting the most accurate and most relevant information to make the best decision possible.

If you are often described as someone who is strong-willed, opinionated, or uncompromising, you're probably not scoring any points on a personal level with your colleagues or with your direct reports. And yes, this also holds true for the most senior company leaders; a company in which the number-one rule is that the boss is always right has a much higher likelihood of failure. The days where organizational success hinged on the lone genius are gone, as one person can't possibly know enough in all the areas needed to achieve sustained success in today's VUCA environment.

Just look at Google, one of the most respected organizations in the world right now. It has been widely publicized (and criticized) that Google allows its people to use 20 percent of their time to work on whatever they want. Google makes this investment because the leaders know that some of the best ideas come from people on the front lines. Instead of making discoveries in a research and development lab, the company essentially has hundreds or thousands of employees working on research and development. It's a much wider net to collect those great ideas on which to base the growth of the company, even if the ideas coming from the employees differ from the ideas coming from the head shed.

Open innovation is a concept that has been around for more than a decade, and it rests on this same foundation of effectiveness, leveraging the diversity of experience. Core to outsmarting VUCA is the idea that unless you create a nonjudgmental environment where the best ideas can bubble to the surface, you run the risk of squashing what could be the next key to your success.

The information in this book can equip C-level execs (CEOs, COOs, CIOs, etc.) with a broader toolset to use in increasing their effectiveness in volatile, uncertain, complex, and ambiguous environments. It can also equip the individual contributor to better recognize fallacies in arguments (their own and others') and then enable them to do something about it. You'll learn to think from different perspectives, consider alternate solutions, and adapt to changing situations. I've also included information, exercises, sample question constructs, and links to web resources that I hope you'll find to be actionable tools for use in your organization.

CULTURAL CHANGE

Let me craft a vision of what your organization will look like if you successfully implement these techniques and processes. Meetings will consist of active debates with assertiveness and open-mindedness and without passive-aggressive resistance or silos. Behind closed doors, many voices will debate vigorously. But once the door opens, one voice will be presented to the public.

The primary focus of the leader is to get as much information as possible from the most diverse group available in order to make the best decision. So while the boss will (hopefully) no longer be the most knowledgeable person in the room, he or she remains responsible and accountable for decisions that are made. The leader also conveys to the team why the decision was made and how the information and different viewpoints that weighed into the decision were valued. Decisions are then reevaluated on a regular basis, without bias, and without succumbing to the preconceived notion of one "right" answer.

That's a picture of the organization of the future that correctly and efficiently outsmarts VUCA. Engaged employees feel like they have a voice at the table, and they begin to understand the rationale the boss uses to make decisions. Employees also have a broader perspective to influence their own decision making and are better able to position their own arguments in light of the larger organizational strategy.

As the leader, you are still accountable in your organization to achieve results; you've got to make the decisions. But with the information in this book, you'll be better equipped to listen, develop your own reasoning skills, and recognize good and faulty arguments so that you can make the best decision possible.

My hope is that by reading this book, you'll learn to think differently, value different perspectives, and leverage the diversity on your team. Outsmarting VUCA is about making the best decision possible given the information available. When you outsmart VUCA, you'll more quickly come to logical conclusions, allowing you to move confidently forward knowing that you have a reasoned, defensible position that is not based on unquestioned assumptions.

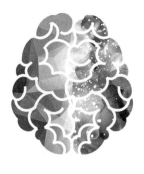

CHAPTER 1

WHAT IS OUTSMARTING VUCA, AND WHY IS IT IMPORTANT?

As a businessperson or individual who needs to make decisions, why should you care about outsmarting VUCA? Just what is "outsmarting VUCA" anyway?

There are a lot of ways to define it, but generally it involves critical thinking or "metacognition"; in other words, you're thinking about thinking. One goal of critical thinking is to be aware of your thoughts and to improve your ability to use reasoned logic, reasoned judgment, and empirical evidence in making the best decision.

Why is outsmarting VUCA important? Because today we all live in a VUCA environment. Almost everything seems to be changing ever more rapidly and the interconnectedness of ideas and concepts is complex. Even when you're able to find those connections, the meaning behind them varies—what means one thing to one person may mean something entirely different to another person. So the reality of our daily environment drives the answer of why outsmarting VUCA is a critical skill to develop today. We simply have to find a way to more effectively interact with this VUCA world.

WHERE DID IT ALL START?

Historically, critical thinking has been around for at least 2,500 years. We can trace the lineage back to Socrates and what came to be known as the Socratic method, a form of discussion that involves stimulating ideas and identifying assumptions through questions and answers. Socrates was of the opinion that faulty reasoning could be uncovered just through disciplined questioning. Did you catch that? Faulty reasoning can be uncovered through disciplined questioning. These same skills can now help us outsmart VUCA.

In school we're often taught to memorize facts, then we're given exams on how well we can recall the information, and then we're graded on our ability to regurgitate what we memorized. Critical thinking is exactly the opposite; it's defined by asking good questions, not by recalling the "right" answer. Critical thinking is beginning to enter the classroom now. But because of all those years it was missing, most of us have not been taught how to think in this way. We spent our school years trying to recall the "right" answer on demand, and now we're in the business world where there often is no "right" answer, just better and worse answers.

It's the same in society. People base their decisions on antiquated models or on assumptions based on their upbringing or cultural realities, etc. These environments often do not exist anymore, and the thinking that people used as they were growing up does not serve them well moving forward.

That's a big problem in a VUCA world: the decisions a person makes are based on data that no longer applies. By definition, what worked yesterday in a VUCA environment won't work tomorrow.

Charles Darwin, one of the greatest critical thinkers in recent history, touted "survival of the fittest" through his theory of evolution. We're evolving into a truly global economy, and companies are facing competition from around the world. A strong competitive advantage in the current market is no longer enough; we must change, adapt, and evolve.

To be effective, that evolution must begin with thinking critically—with getting better at asking the right questions. Instead of coming up with answers and hanging onto them long after they're applicable, we need to continually ask: How do we know this answer is still true? What new information do we have that could affect our earlier decisions? By asking good questions, we'll come to better answers. And asking good questions forms the foundation we'll need to outsmart VUCA.

THE VALUE OF DIVERSITY

People with different backgrounds and experiences have different points of view and, consequently, approach situations differently.

Only a few generations ago, it was common for the majority of people to spend their entire lives in one small area, their tasks slowly evolving independent of outside-world influence.

Today's mobility and access to information exposes us to different ways of doing things, to different ways of thinking. We share ideas, experiences, and best practices, and the amount of data that we have available to us has never been greater in the history of mankind.

This added complexity is a good thing, but it can also be paralyzing without a framework to use in evaluating the information. As a result, in the face of this enormous complexity, we tend to rely on our own experiences, which lead us to judge the behaviors of others as being "strange." And to the degree that we remain centered on our own way of doing things, we miss incredible opportunities to do things differently, some of which may actually be more appropriate for the specific challenge that we're currently facing.

That's the value of diversity, and today we have incredible opportunities to leverage it. Instead of just assuming why people act the way they do, we must reflect on the diverse experiences we're exposed to and gain some understanding of the behaviors of others. Let me give you an example from my experience.

When I speak at conferences and events in Asian countries it's not uncommon for me to see someone in public wearing a white surgical-type mask. For many years, I interpreted that sight as being an individual who is concerned about getting sick from germs or breathing polluted air. After many years of making that assumption without checking the validity of it, I finally learned that the person wearing the surgical mask is often sick herself and doesn't want to spread her germs to others. She is wearing the mask not as a form of defense but as a form of consideration. That's part of a collective culture's mind-set. For someone from an individualistic culture, like America, it's fairly easy to misconstrue the behavior of someone from a collective culture. That's why there's value in being exposed to diversity. It's a chance to reflect on the experience and gain some understanding of the motivation behind the behaviors of others.

Too often, we quickly climb the "Ladder of Inference," a concept formulated by Harvard Business School professor Chris Argyris as a way of explaining how people view the world around them, interpret selected data, and come rapidly to their conclusions. The lowest rung of the ladder is the observation rung, where relevant information is gathered. That's the level we need to force ourselves back to—that observation level—especially when we find ourselves making unsubstantiated assumptions or when our conclusion differs significantly from someone with a different cultural background than ours. Look at the observable data instead of the meanings ascribed to the data, and then ask yourself, "What else could the data mean?" Exposure to diversity forces us to confront different interpretations of the exact same data. Diversity is an invaluable asset when outsmarting VUCA.

Back in 1999, ABC's *Nightline* news program challenged IDEO, a product development company in the San Francisco Bay Area, to redesign a grocery shopping cart in five days. The group used a process called the "Deep Dive," in which the members of the IDEO team behave almost like cultural anthropologists, pretending they are on completely unfamiliar turf. Instead of *déjà vu,* where you are in an unfamiliar situation but it feels very familiar, the IDEO team practices the inverse, or *vuja de,* where they are in a familiar situation but treat it as if it's their first time. One of the key success criteria for the Deep Dive is to ensure the maximum amount of diversity on the IDEO team. This allows for a richness of dialogue and a diversity of perspectives.

That's outsmarting VUCA at its core. It's looking at a familiar situation in a different light and from a different perspective (or two or five). How can you go into the same situation every day and yet be open to "seeing" it in new ways? When you're exposed to different cultures, how do you interpret the unique behaviors while being fully aware of your own cultural filters affecting their interpretation?

By seeing things from different perspectives, you get a more complete view of the situation. It's like the fable of the blind men who were trying to describe an elephant. One held onto the tail and described it as most like a rope, another touched the ear and described it as most like a hand fan, a third felt the elephant's leg and described it as most like a pillar, and so on. All of them were right, and yet in some versions of the story they violently disagreed because they were not open to the diverse (and equally correct) viewpoints of the other blind men.

BEING CHALLENGED

Outsmarting VUCA challenges us to step back from the situation and realize that there may be more going on than what we initially thought. It challenges us to try to see life from other perspectives instead of just hanging on tightly to our own unexamined or unchallenged belief systems.

The philosopher Arthur Schopenhauer said, "All truth passes through three stages. First, it is ridiculed. Second, it is violently opposed. Third, it is accepted as being self-evident." When we're questioning beliefs, we usually find ourselves in one of these three stages. After the initial ridicule, the idea gains some traction and then violent opposition begins, often by people who take it as a threat to their own self-image—we've seen this throughout history in people whose religious beliefs are foundational to who they are. We've also witnessed the third stage of Schopenhauer's statement—it hasn't been long that the truth of the Earth as round moved from being violently opposed to being self-evident, as it is today..

Try as we might, however, we'll never truly get rid of our "baggage." That's not the ultimate goal of critical thinking. Instead, it's about being aware of who we are and understanding that we are products of our culture and environment. Without the experiences and traits that make us unique, we would have homogeneity—that's the biggest enemy of effective group-level critical thinking. If everyone thinks the same way, "groupthink" happens. Our individual baggage is the unique value that we bring to the table. But we need to understand how that baggage (our experiences over a lifetime) impacts our thinking, our rationalization, and the way we come to decisions.

Doris Kearns Goodwin, the world-renowned presidential historian and Pulitzer Prize-winning author of *Team of Rivals: The Political Genius of Abraham Lincoln*, speaks about the value of surrounding yourself with people who think differently than you. President Lincoln, for example, surrounded himself with advisors, several of whom were his chief rivals from the recent presidential campaign, men who were more popular than Lincoln and who were also great thinkers. At the time, Lincoln knew that the country needed the best and the brightest to solve its problems, and he knew of no one brighter than the men he "hired" to be his advisors.

It takes a lot of self-awareness and confidence to surround yourself with people that you know are going to challenge your thinking. That is key to outsmarting VUCA. Surrounding yourself with "yes men" is the antithesis of outsmarting VUCA;

Do not surround yourself with people who think the same way you do if you want to make the best decisions possible. that's not how to evolve and make progress.

In a rapidly changing VUCA environment, developing a deep understanding of others is critical to survival, regardless of where they live and how diverse their desires are.

· ·

Do not surround yourself with people who think the same way you do if you want to make the best decisions possible.

· ·

One of my clients, the Cheesecake Factory, is a good example of this on the corporate level. I have been continually impressed that the company's menus are customized to the region in which the company operates. You can always get basic cheesecake and other staples, but in the Middle Eastern market, for example, the menu complies with Islamic dietary laws, and in Mexico the company works hard to ensure that the food is culturally authentic. By outsmarting VUCA, the Cheesecake Factory strategically moved toward "mass customization" on top of the basics, which allowed for effective and efficient regionalization instead of just the mass production and standardization that defines so many of their competitors.

. . . .

CRITICAL THINKING
EXPERIMENT

In an experiment I ran with a Fortune 100 company, I created a fictitious culture in which members of a group could not communicate with each other unless they were touching. If a member of the group broke contact with the others, it was considered rude. The other members of the group would then just ignore the person who broke contact—they would behave as if they couldn't "hear" the person who wasn't touching.

Then I brought in people in the role of civil engineers, and they were assigned to help the people in the culture group learn how to build a bridge across a deep ravine. But the engineers didn't know anything about the fictitious culture; they didn't know that people in the culture group had to be touching the person who was trying to communicate with them. The job of the engineers was to outsmart VUCA to figure out how to interact with the people in the culture group and teach them how to build a bridge.

One particularly memorable gentleman in the engineer role had figured out some of the behavior, so he was touching the shoulders of two women who were in the culture group and was succeeding in giving them instructions. Then one of the two women had to bend over to diagram the bridge on a piece of paper, and in doing so, she broke contact with the engineer.

The engineer was still touching the arm of the standing woman in the culture group, but he was talking to the woman who had bent over and was drawing. Of course, per the rules of the simulation, the woman drawing couldn't hear the engineer because he wasn't touching her. The engineer kept trying to instruct the woman that she was drawing the lines incorrectly, but she just kept drawing because in her culture she couldn't hear him since he wasn't touching her. All the while, the engineer was getting angrier and angrier.

In an effort to not lose the learning goal of the simulation (and to avoid the impending cardiac arrest!), I gently intervened and asked the standing woman in the culture group to give the engineer a little hint regarding this unique behavior of touching while communicating. So the standing woman discretely said to the engineer, "Um, she can't hear you."
The engineer acknowledged the instructions as if a lightbulb had illuminated and then leaned over close to the drawing woman's ear and proceeded to yell the instructions at her,

which understandably frightened the woman and ended the simulation.

This demonstrates how we filter data and create our own assumptions. As soon as the engineer received a piece of information, he interpreted it through his own lens, his own filter. *If she can't hear me*, he thought, *it must mean that I'm not talking loudly enough.* Of course, the problem was indeed that she couldn't hear the engineer. But the solution, according to her culture, was not to talk louder but to touch her while talking to her so that she could hear.

. . . .

Every business needs to follow this practice if it wants to compete on a global scale. Instead of assuming what will work in a culture, use the processes outlined in this book to ask questions and figure out how to remain true to your core offerings and still adapt to the environment. And remember that culture shifts— it's always moving. So you'll miss opportunities and become antiquated if you keep doing things the way you've always done them.

Just look at the eleven companies profiled in Jim Collins' book *Good to Great*. Having made the transition from good to great, many of the companies profiled are now either bankrupt or have been acquired by much larger (and presumably healthier) companies. If you do not continue to outsmart

VUCA, your business will not survive. It's crucial in business to make decisions purposefully, and to do that, you and your team need to think differently.

THE BLIND SPOT

Nobel Prize-winning biologist Peter Medawar said, "Never fall in love with your hypothesis." That gets to the essence of the challenge that outsmarting VUCA addresses at a personal level. If you are so in love with your own theories, then you may not be open to alternative ways of doing things.

A pastor friend of mine once asked me, "If I could prove to you beyond a shadow of a doubt that your faith was misplaced, would you denounce your belief?" Sure, I'd like to think I would, but that would call into question everything that I believed; I'd have to reorder my entire belief system in order to do so. But if I didn't change my beliefs—if I was unwilling to accept the proof that my beliefs were wrong—then I wouldn't be a logical, rational thinker. So the correct answer had to be yes, I would change my beliefs. In light of evidence, you must be willing to change your beliefs. That's a hallmark of someone willing and able to outsmart VUCA.

But that's also the challenge—asking someone to change their belief system or to rework their mental models. It's much easier to rely on rationalizations such as "because I said so" or "because it's always been that way." True critical thinking overcomes the opposition and asks good questions to produce even better answers.

At a personal level, it's challenging to change beliefs not only because it goes against the grain but also because we have our own blind spots—the complete lack of awareness that another way of thinking exists. We're not even aware that someone could think differently than us.

As I speak around the world, it's always fascinating to me what people eat. For example, on a recent trip to Peru, I learned that a fairly common dish in Peru is cuy (pronounced kwee), or guinea pig, which at a visceral level is repulsive to many people from North American cultures where guinea pigs are considered pets. They're sold in pet stores, not grocery stores. Conversely, Peruvians undoubtedly find many of the foods North Americans eat repulsive. These reactions are not due to logic, as there's no right or wrong. But without understanding and accepting that cultures are different, it's easy to jump to a harsh conclusion about a person or group's relative level of refinement or maturity.

Interpreting information in that harsh light, through your own preconceived ideas around "right" and "wrong," is an example of a common blind spot. You don't even know that you're doing it; you assume that your way is the only (right) way. Consequently, you misinterpret another culture's actions as being abnormal. You may even pass judgment to the point of deciding you could never do business with anyone of that culture. If you do that, you severely limit your ability to grow. Outsmarting VUCA requires accepting someone's differences as interesting enough to want to learn more. That's how progress is made in a VUCA environment.

Think about it from the perspective of a simple goldfish. Swimming around in its bowl, the goldfish is problem free. It doesn't realize this lack of problems has anything to do with the water it is swimming in—until you take the water away. If you're never pulled out of your fishbowl, you have no frame of reference for knowing that there is something outside the water.

PURPOSEFUL EXPOSURE

Travel is a great way to expose yourself and your blind spots to opportunities to develop the skills necessary to outsmart VUCA, but it should be done systematically and purposefully.

To outsmart VUCA, you must expose yourself to different cultures and experiences and then ask, "What are they doing that's better than what I do?" or "How can I take what they do, integrate it with what I do, and actually come up with a third solution that's even better?"

As an engineer, I like things orderly. But periodically I schedule at least a week or two where I deliberately put myself into an uncomfortable situation. A few years ago, I traveled to Peru for the first time. I didn't speak the language, and I purposely didn't do any research beforehand. I kept a journal of the trip so that I could reflect later.

At one point, I wanted to go to Machu Picchu and had no idea how to get there. Using broken language and gestures to get directions, I ended up on a bus that I hoped would take me there. As is apparently common there, people were standing inside the bus and hanging on the outside. I had a chicken on my lap and there was a goat standing in the center aisle. It was chaos topped by travel over incredibly rough roads.

Afterward, I reflected on what I wrote in my journal about the experience. I recorded it as being uncomfortable and a situation I couldn't wait to escape. But why did it make me uncomfortable? No one else seemed uncomfortable; for them, it was nothing out of the ordinary. Yet for me, it was way outside my comfort zone. Why? By reflecting on it, I was able to examine the experience and gain some new insights about myself. Not until I took myself out of my comfortable fishbowl did I realize that area of my goldfish-ness.

. . . .

GET OUT OF YOUR FISHBOWL

By traveling, you open yourself up to opportunity to interact with people from different cultures who do things that make no sense to you whatsoever.

I had the privilege of living in Germany for a few years. In much of Europe, it's very common for grocery stores to be closed on Sunday. For the most part, you buy groceries almost daily, in part because the refrigerators are very small by American standards. But I come from a culture where it is common to do grocery shopping on the weekend, and sometimes in bulk, for the entire week or even weeks ahead. One Saturday, we'd been invited to a wedding of a couple friends we'd made while there. She was Ukrainian, and he was Russian. With the wedding starting at 11 a.m. Saturday morning, I planned on doing our grocery shopping afterward, knowing that nothing would be open on Sunday. By my frame of reference, we should be finished with the wedding by 1 p.m. or maybe 2 p.m. at the latest. But I learned the hard way that wedding celebrations differ considerably across cultures. At 10 p.m. Saturday evening, we were the first to leave. The festivities went well into the next day.

How inefficient, I thought. The wedding experience and Sunday grocery store closing (we missed getting groceries that weekend) exposed two preconceived notions, or blind spots, of mine.

It took me years of living over there not only to notice the differences of that culture but to appreciate them. In fact, my wife and I planned on bringing that "Sunday-day-of-rest" culture back with us when we repatriated. Unfortunately, it only lasted about a month, since we quickly assimilated back to a seven-day-a-week culture in America.

. . . .

Most of my Fortune 500 corporate clients send their up-and-coming executives overseas on temporary expatriate assignments to expose them to a culture other than their own. However, internationally acclaimed psychologist and lecturer Daniel Goleman says in his book *Emotional Intelligence* that before you can regulate your own reactions you have to be aware of your own emotions; in other words, self-awareness precedes self-regulation. So the deliberate expatriate assignment for top execs or the similar mandatory high school foreign culture study is worth little if the traveler doesn't grow, reflect, and have some resulting level of self-awareness of his or her blind spots.

Today, in the United States, we're in the fortunate position of being able to gain cultural exposure without leaving the country because of pockets of different cultural groups across the nation. For example, on a recent speaking engagement in Michigan, I read about a large concentration of Muslims who had recently immigrated to the United States and settled as a group in the Dearborn area. Why? Perhaps because they, like most of us, tend to be most comfortable among people with similar backgrounds and behaviors. We tend to gravitate toward people who are like us because it's familiar, it's comfortable. We don't have to think about adapting, because their rules are our rules.

To really outsmart VUCA as an individual, you must purposefully put yourself in uncomfortable situations so that you can challenge your thinking, find your blind spots, and shift your vision to a new perspective.

GENERATIONAL DIFFERENCES

Generational differences are possibly the most underleveraged source of diversity that we have at our fingertips. In many of the global organizations with which I work, I often encourage teams that really want to outsmart VUCA to have someone from each of the generations—baby boomers, Gen X, and millennials—represented on their team, because the different generations (as we define them) very often have a certain way of approaching problems, situations, and challenges.

For instance, my grandparents emigrated from England when my dad was about eight years old. They came from a very poor part of England near Manchester, a coal-mining town where the prevalence of black lung disease meant the average life span was less than forty-five years.

In America, my grandfather worked as a welder. He retired in the 1970s, and then my grandparents moved to Santa Barbara to be closer to my father and our family. They lived very frugally here; their house was a mobile home, they drove an old Toyota Camry, and my grandmother reused tea bags three or four times.

When they got to be in their eighties, we had to look for other options for their living arrangements because they couldn't really live on their own anymore. But it was thousands of dollars monthly for any type of assisted living in the Santa Barbara area. While they kept their financial situation private, we knew they didn't have much money, so we had a difficult heart-to-heart talk with them and let them know that, because of their financial situation, they may need to move in with my family.

They were a bit embarrassed and agreed that, yes, they didn't have a lot of money. But when they showed us their bank passbook, well, let's just say we were shocked! They had done an exceptional job of saving over the years. But that was fairly typical of people in their generation. They had been raised in a different time, and as a result they had a different view of prosperity—a kind of a "waste not, want not" attitude. By the way, we told grandma it was okay to stop reusing teabags three times (although she never did change).

The way we live today compared to how my grandparents lived their lives is not right or wrong, it's just different.

There's a lot of value in cross-generational diversity when it comes to outsmarting VUCA.

Today, where older generations may be offended by someone taking a phone call in the middle of a conversation, younger generations think nothing of interrupting talk by answering a text. At any Starbucks or college campus, kids sit across the table from each other texting and talking at the same time. In fact, sometimes they're texting the person right across the table from them! They don't think it rude not to verbally converse; to them, texting each other is a perfectly acceptable and appropriate way of interacting. In fact, many of them reading this book right now are saying, "Wait, that's not appropriate?"

We used to be fearful that the Internet age would bring about "cocooning"—we'd all be homebound because everything would be delivered and we wouldn't need to go out. There was a fear that our kids were going to be antisocial, that they weren't going to know how to interact with others. To a large degree, that really hasn't materialized. In some ways, younger generations are even more social than the older generations were at their age because they have access to and are using multiple modes of communication. Many of them have a much bigger network of "friends." Again, not right or wrong, just different.

But what does this mean? It means they're going to approach relationships differently. They have different wants and needs in life. They tend to be more fluid and more comfortable with technology.

There are a lot of generalizations about the generations currently in the workforce. Certainly there are exceptions, but generally speaking there are some significant differences in how you process information depending on your generation or in what part of the United States or world you were raised.

Generational differences are significantly underestimated for their value in bringing diversity of opinion to a group. In cultures where age is revered, the opinions and ideas of the younger generation are often belittled, when in reality they need to be embraced.

It's the same in cultures where age is not revered; seniors have valid ideas as well and should not be discounted.

Earlier I mentioned IDEO, the product development company. IDEO's teams are very diverse—they're cross-cultural, cross-generational groups. As a result, the company is creating an environment where the best decisions can be made not without friction but through productive conflict.

There's a lot of data out there suggesting that the empowered team will almost always outperform the lone genius. That's our new VUCA environment today and for the foreseeable future.

THE IMPORTANCE OF ROLES

Becoming better at outsmarting VUCA is about forcing yourself to examine your own thoughts in order to discover how you come to certain conclusions. But it's also about looking at a situation not just from your own perspective but also from others.

This is where the concept of roles comes into play. Roles allow for better decision making as an individual and allow for a respectfully confrontational approach to critical thinking when working in teams.

Earlier I mentioned the concept of "groupthink." This is when the blind spots of individuals reinforce a group's blind spots. That's why diversity in groups is valuable—because it helps expose blind spots. With diversity, someone in the group inevitably thinks of something that others in the group never even considered.

For example, let's say I put together a focus group to gather information about reactions to a certain product. If I include a twentysomething in the group, obviously I'm looking for input from the twentysomething perspective from that person. If that person starts trying to contribute from a fiftysomething perspective, she is not adding her unique value to the group.

This is one of the main purposes of focus groups—to capture the diversity of the market. If we have a focus group that's homogenous, we run the risk of not addressing the needs of the market segments that are absent from the group.

It's the same with teams working to make a decision. In order to get them to outsmart VUCA, they must be made up of people who think differently, who can play different roles in the thinking process (a team of rivals, so to speak): Who's the antagonist? Who's the optimist? Who's going to keep asking, "How do we know that?" If your team is homogenous, then the various roles need to be simulated. I'll talk about this more in chapter five.

For the individual, processing a situation from the perspective of various roles can seem almost schizophrenic. It's about role-playing systematically, linearly, sequentially. This is a skill that's difficult to develop, but one of the purposes of this book is to show you what roles are key, generally speaking, for getting that diversity of thought to make sure you, as an individual, are outsmarting VUCA as effectively as you can.

Today's workplaces are filled with people who do not use critical thinking. Faulty reasoning incurs increased damage in today's fast-changing workplace.

In the pages that follow, we'll go through different ways of allowing you to recognize your own blind spots, of forcing you out of your own framework into a different framework. It's role-playing in a more systematic way so that, at the end of the process, you're sure that you've done everything you can to make the best decision possible.

TAKEAWAYS

1. Reflect on some of the uncomfortable experiences you've encountered recently. What do you better understand now about the person or instance that contributed to your discomfort?

2. What will you commit to doing in order to proactively expose your blind spots?

3. Consider your last travel experience. What did you learn about the people in the location, beyond just superficial differences?

4. What is your role at work? In life? And in that role, what can you uniquely contribute to your team, or to each decision-making situation? What is your unique perspective?

Visit the Institute for the Advancement of Critical Thinking, www.theiact.org, for more information on VUCA basics.

CHAPTER 2

COMMON ERRORS IN THINKING

We've established the need and the value of outsmarting VUCA, and in this chapter we'll talk about the faults or fallacies in our own arguments and in the arguments of others.

For now, let's talk about the errors we sometimes have in our own internal processes and how they impact our thinking. We will also learn how to recognize these in others, but for now let's focus on how to recognize these internal or psychological factors in our own thought processes.

In order to begin practicing and strengthening your ability to outsmart VUCA, you must first be aware of errors in your own thinking. Once you recognize these errors in yourself, then you can determine what you should do about them.

Earlier, we discussed the concept of blind spots. We all have these, and they're most easily exposed when someone else weighs in and affects our thinking. The problem is that often we don't give people that opportunity to weigh in. People have definitive opinions because often they believe, sometimes subconsciously, that there is only one way of doing things. That opinion is usually based on our own internal processes, and without examining those processes and finding the blind spots, we don't recognize the errors in our thinking. We don't discover the internal psychological factors that are related to our own assumptions, biases, and beliefs.

In fact, there's a great quote by Diane Halpern in her book *Thought and Knowledge: An Introduction to Critical Thinking.* Halpern writes, "The fact is that in our everyday thinking, the psychological processes quite often are not logical. . . We alter information we are given according to our beliefs and then decide if a conclusion follows from the altered information. We function under a kind of personal logic." I could not agree more.

So what is this "personal logic" that Halpern writes about? That's when you unknowingly alter the information to fit your experience, or framework, and then come to your own conclusions. To correct the problem, you must "unalter" the information, and the best way to do that is to become aware of your own internal thinking . . . and then actively challenge it.

BIAS AND SELF-AWARENESS

Bias is that internal framework, the internal beliefs that people don't even realize they have. Bias may be based on culture, upbringing, mind-set, or even emotions, and it is often triggered by specific words or behaviors.

When making an argument, people who are very skilled at rhetoric use trigger words to get a response. For example, back in the USSR days, a mention of the word "communist" would immediately trigger an emotional response from many in the Western world. Similarly, during the reign of the Third Reich, you'd get an immediate reaction if you mentioned Hitler or Nazis. Other trigger words? Trigger words today might include abortion, fundamentalism, Islam, and Democrat/Republican/Libertarian. These and other words often cause an immediate, visceral reaction in many people, positive or negative, which signals the existence of biases.

According to current research, we can never truly get rid of all our biases. However, you can begin to develop the discipline to think through your biases and to search out data and opinions that directly conflict with your own view of the world. To do that, you must begin by being aware of your own biases.

While there's value in knowing where your biases come from, understanding where they originate is not essential to outsmarting VUCA. For example, perhaps you recognize that you have an issue with authority; for whatever reason, whenever you encounter someone in authority, you immediately distrust that person. The key for outsmarting VUCA is to recognize this and other biases you possess and then ensure that they don't negatively impact your ability to make the best decision possible.

Where that bias comes from is a much deeper issue and beyond the scope of this book.

Please don't misunderstand me. I'm not saying you must rid yourself of all biases. That may be a worthwhile goal and the subject of many other books. The goal of this book is to enable you to be aware of your biases so that they don't cause you to make flawed decisions.

In fact, sometimes biases can work in a person's favor. For example, emotions can be a real asset when passion is needed to sell a product or service, but it can be a little overwhelming when input is needed for a strategic decision in an organization. Engineers tend to be rather analytical—that's a plus if you need an in-depth review of data, but it's not so great if you need a hug. People and their biases are often well suited to one situation but not another.

Again, this is not about removing biases; it's about being aware of them so that you know what you and others bring to the table in a given situation. Remember: diversity is one of the main tactics of outsmarting VUCA in a group.

As psychologist Daniel Goleman says in *Emotional Intelligence*, it's about self-awareness and then self-regulation: first you've got to be self-aware, and then you've got to regulate your behavior and take steps to ensure your biases are not negatively impacting your decision making.

If you can grow, learn, and become more balanced, that's great, but you'll never be starting from a blank piece of paper.

We are all products of our environment, and with that uniqueness comes certain biases.

Here are nine of the more common biases, or errors, in reasoning. All of these are related to each other, some more than others, and it's not uncommon for us (and others) to employ more than one at a time. As you're going through the list, honestly and patiently reflect on them to identify and address which of these biases impact your own thinking.

Bias #1: Clouding the issue with extremes. Sometimes known as "the atmospheric effect," this bias involves using all-encompassing words and phrases like "all," "none," "No one could actually believe that," or "Everybody already knows that." We say these to ourselves when internally processing information. They are not necessarily true, but we take them at face value and then formulate statements based on that atmospheric effect.

This kind of thinking leads to faulty conclusions that are not necessarily supported by the evidence.

For example, in the San Francisco Bay Area in California, say there is a belief that if you work at a tech company, you live in the suburbs, but not if you're the founder of the company—no Internet entrepreneur would be caught dead living in the suburbs. Now, if you also assumed that everyone who lives in the suburbs shops at strip malls, then you might say it follows logically that no Internet entrepreneurs shop at strip malls.

Does that follow logically? Think it through! Essentially, the argument boils down to "No Internet entrepreneur lives in the suburbs," and "All people who live in the suburbs shop at strip malls," hence "No Internet entrepreneurs shop at strip malls." It's actually a faulty conclusion based on clouding the issue with extremes like "none of these people" and "all of these people" phrases. Even if the two statements are accepted as true, the resulting conclusion doesn't logically follow.

If you were in a group and someone made this argument, it would surely beg you to think, *I can think of examples where that's not true.*

Even statements like "everybody who lives in the suburbs shops at strip malls" are faulty. What about the people who live in suburbs but never set foot in strip malls?

"All" or "none" statements make for faulty arguments inside your brain. In this instance, you're assuming that nobody outside of the suburbs shops at strip malls. That's obviously a false statement.

However, if you had the data to prove your point—that no Internet executives live in the suburbs and *only* people who live in the suburbs shop at strip malls—then you could logically say that "no Internet executives shop at strip malls."

Additionally, the phrase "everybody who lives in the suburbs shops at strip malls" could be true without necessarily excluding the Internet executives—for instance, if the Internet execs lived in the hills and yet still shopped at strip malls.

However you slice it, it's convoluted logic that clouds the issue by using terms like "no" or "all" or "everyone." Each statement can be individually true, and yet their combination doesn't logically support the conclusion.

This fallacy can take you to a dangerous place in business.

For example, when I was in high school, I managed a gift store that sold stuffed animals; that's all it sold. It was a great store located in one of the nicer Santa Barbara strip malls. People would routinely spend $100 to $150 on stuffed animals. Around the holidays, the store made $2,000 to $3,000 an hour selling stuffed animals. Back in the early eighties, this was a lot of money!

Then the owner decided that he wanted to expand, and in looking for a potential location, he chose the fastest-growing city in California at the time—Bakersfield. He wanted to be where the action was, so he leased a space in a new strip mall there. His logic, simplified, went something like this: "All of my sales come through people shopping at the mall. No one buys my stuffed animals unless they are at the mall. Therefore, to grow sales, I need to open a store in the fastest-growing mall in the area."

In less than two years, he had to close both stores. The Bakersfield store was a flop. Why? He failed to recognize the atmospheric effect. Yes, Bakersfield was the fastest-growing city, but the customer demographic was completely different than in Santa Barbara. Bakersfield was largely growing due to the influx of working-class people, not people who would spend $150 of disposable income on stuffed animals.

So being in the "fastest-growing" mall and having increased foot traffic did not link directly to success in selling stuffed animals. His flawed logic got in the way of realizing that the customer's amount of disposable income was more directly linked to the store's success.

The dangerous piece is that, once in a while, people get lucky and succeed in spite of faulty logic. This is one reason some people irrationally choose to ignore logic.

Bias #2: It's always been that way, therefore it will always be that way. Often referred to as "belief bias," this fallacy is about importing data from your past into your present, assuming the situation will be the same the next time you encounter it. Obviously, this is dangerous because things change, especially in a VUCA environment.

Often, people draw conclusions based on data that appear to be related when viewed with certain assumptions. Taken independently, however, the data are actually not related. The key here is to view the data with a fresh perspective, not through the lens of past experiences, in order to remove the complexity and ambiguity.

A statement often heard in business is: "Well, that's the way things are done here," or "That's the way we've always done it." But just because something has been done a certain way doesn't mean that it's the best way or the only way to do it. There may be a better way.

. . . .

CHANGING BIASES OVER TIME

There was a time when a man appearing on television in a white coat and giving out health-care advice had immediate credibility. Obviously, he's a doctor, we thought. He must know what he's talking about because doctors are really smart. They've gone to school for a long time, and they can be trusted.

In reality, he was probably just a paid actor, and what we were watching was just a marketing ploy.

Nowadays, according to various studies, younger generations are naturally more skeptical. They tend to believe that someone's always trying to sell them something because that's the environment in which they have been raised. Now when someone in a white coat appears on a TV commercial, there's more likely to be distrust toward that person because we recognize that he or she is probably a paid actor impersonating a doctor. The advertisers are taking advantage of our biases, and they're trying to sell us something. Their goal doesn't change as our biases change—just their tactics. This is a good example of how biases change over time.

Consider how collective blind spots, resulting from bias, have changed over time. For example, a father and son are riding their bikes down the street. A car pulls out and hits the son. The boy is injured. The father tends to his son, calls 911, and an ambulance comes to take the boy to the hospital. The father crawls in the back of the ambulance and rides along.

In the emergency room, the father is told the son needs surgery right away, but he (the father) must wait in the waiting room. The father returns to the waiting room, and the boy gets rushed into surgery.

The surgeon approaches the table to operate on the boy, takes one look at the boy's face and pulls back, saying, "I can't operate on this boy, he's my son."

How can that be?

In posing this riddle to groups twenty years ago, the participants were perplexed. I don't know, they'd think, how is this possible? The surgeon must have made a mistake; maybe the boy just looks like his son.

The now-obvious answer, of course, is that the surgeon is his mother.

Note: Today, this is an even more difficult riddle to use because the audience either immediately guesses the surgeon is the boy's mother, or they think the boy does indeed have two fathers. Either way, it exposes biases.

Not that many years ago, it was highly unusual for a woman to be a surgeon; the vast majority of surgeons were men. And in the past, the boy's parents would have been a man and woman; today, he could easily have two fathers, stepparents, etc.

When it comes to family, our culture has shifted so dramatically in the last twenty years that there are many different answers to this riddle, each equally valid.

But this example does raise some good questions: What will our world be like twenty years from now? How antiquated will our biases today seem to people in the not-so-distant future?

• •

A classic example of this is the story of the newlyweds. In this story, the wife decides to make a roast beef dinner for her new husband. She buys a roast, places it in a pan, cuts off the ends of the roast, and then cooks it in the oven. The husband, watching this, says, "Why do you cut off both ends of the roast?" The wife answers, "What do you mean? That's the way you make a roast." He says, "I've never seen it done that way," and she replies, "Well, that's the way my mother did it."

The next time they go to a family dinner with the wife's family, the wife makes a roast and takes it along. The husband looks for the first opportunity to politely ask his mother-in-law, "Why do you cut off both ends of the roast before cooking it? I've never seen it done that way." The mother-in-law replies, "Well, that's the way you make a roast. That's the way I was taught by my mother. Grandma is here, let's ask her."

So they ask the grandmother, who says, "Wait, you cut off the ends of your roast? For the love of . . . I only cut off the ends because the roast wouldn't fit in my pan."

A family tradition had been going on for generations, and no one knew why; it's just the way they had been taught.

An example of belief bias from my own experience involves a girl I attended high school with. Back then, she was very open about her desire to marry into money. She didn't want to work a day in her life. Her future husband's only qualification was that he had to be rich. If a guy asked her out, she would ask him where he lived, what kind of car his parents drove, etc. She was very deliberate, even in high school, about whom she even dated.

I never saw her after graduation, and she didn't come to the ten-year reunion. But at that reunion, someone commented that of course she wouldn't show up, because she had married some entrepreneur, a multimillionaire. She got her wish. She had her plan, and we all agreed that she executed it perfectly. That's belief bias—we couldn't possibly believe that she married the guy out of love. She had said what she was going to do, and with just one other piece of data—that she did indeed marry a multimillionaire—our beliefs were confirmed that she married him just because of his money.

We don't know for certain that was the truth, but we took those two pieces of data and came to a conclusion that may or may not be true.

The solution comes when you seek out alternate viewpoints and challenge your own blind spots. In this example, if we ran across her in a few years and we found out that she married her husband when he was penniless, we might still be tempted to jump to a conclusion that validates our past beliefs—that she's lying or that she knew it was just a matter of time until he became rich.

Encountering contradictory data once you have a particular belief leads to cognitive dissonance. It requires changing your mental model (or ignoring the contradictory data). Changing a mental model is uncomfortable to do, and it takes a lot of work for most of us.

The belief bias is about importing past data into a future decision without knowing if the past data even applies to the situation and without actively searching for information that would prove your beliefs false.

Bias #3: Wishful thinking. This bias is about believing that something will happen just because you really want it to. In other words, you're fooling yourself, and when the facts really become known, you're almost embarrassed—that's a good litmus test for this fallacy of reasoning.

This commonly happens in business research and development. Often an organization's leaders just know if they spend enough money on a product, everything will work out in the end. Maybe they have friends who all say they want one, so they believe everyone's going to want one. But where is the data to back that up? What are the facts? Even if friends all say they'll want one, that's relying on an insufficient sample size (see Bias #8) and a host of other biases.

Wishful thinking is almost intentional blindness. It's choosing to focus only on things that reinforce your existing beliefs because you almost have a hunch that asking questions will reveal data that you don't want to acknowledge.

There are countless stories of ideas that never launched because of insufficient sample size or not doing enough market research. Even the product development company IDEO has a few war stories. In one example, the company developed a product that would help kids tie their shoes—colorful, attention-getting rubber monsters that tied into the shoelaces. The product failed miserably. It was a cool product, but nobody wanted it. Wishful thinking led to the belief that if they built the product, everyone would want one.

I'm guilty of wishful thinking myself. Years ago, I invested in a company that put up satellites that would allow a person to talk on a phone anywhere in the world without any dropped calls. In the middle of the ocean, the desert, the forest, with no cell tower around, you'd still be able to get good coverage and make phone calls.

I thought the company was going to be huge, so I invested. This is my retirement, I thought, everyone was going to want one of these phones. It never dawned on me that, in reality, very few people need to make a phone call in the middle of the ocean or the desert. The company failed miserably, and I ended up losing my investment. If I had looked more closely at the facts, it would have been painfully obvious that I was relying on wishful thinking. But because I was enamored with the technology and what a cool idea it was, I didn't even choose to look at the data.

Bias #4: Confirmation bias. This is about looking only at evidence that supports a decision you've made or a conclusion you want to reach. It's really only looking for confirmation of what you already believe.

For example, let's say I believe that the way to become financially independent is to start your own company. Indeed, in looking at data for the top fifty richest people in America, I realize that many got rich from starting a company and making a truckload of money. Bill Gates, Warren Buffett, Steve Jobs, I just go down the list. Therefore, I'm going to quit my job and start my own company, and then I'm going to get rich.

I'm ignoring the data that says nine out of ten start-ups fail within the first five years. That's uncomfortable. I don't look at that data, because I only want to look for evidence that supports the conclusion I've already reached or that supports the decision I've already made.

Confirmation bias is one of the most common biases, and it's a dangerous one because it openly ignores, downplays, or dismisses any contradictory information.

. . . .

MY BROTHER, THE PROBATION OFFICER

For the past twenty-eight years, my brother has worked as a juvenile probation officer.

At any given time, he has dozens of juvenile offenders under his authority, wending their way through the system. Over the years, he has explained to me that they prefer to keep juveniles who are on probation and from the same family together under the same probation officer. My brother gets to know these families quite well, especially when they have multiple children in the system. It turns out, interventions that consider family dynamics are much more likely to succeed long term than those that ignore family dynamics.

In one case, my brother got to know the family of a teenage girl who was part of his caseload. During one visit, he met this girl's younger brother, who was already beginning to get involved with gangs, even at eleven or twelve years old. So, trying not to be fatalistic, my brother knew the chances were good that the younger brother would eventually end up in his caseload.

Sure enough, he walked in one morning and there was the younger brother's file. Oddly, my brother's boss phoned him as soon as he arrived at work to make sure he had seen the file. His boss explained that the principal of the school wanted special attention paid to the boy because he wasn't a bad kid, just truant—he wouldn't go to school. If my brother could get him back in school, the principal reasoned, the boy had good friends there who would keep him out of trouble and out of the gangs. My brother affirmed that he understood, all while noting that usually his boss didn't call him on cases, so he knew that this case was special.

That morning also happened to be the one day of the week that juvenile probation officers went before the judge to go through their cases and recommend probation sentencing.

My brother went to court and was waiting his turn to present to the judge when he noticed a group of gang members in the back of the courtroom. This wasn't an uncommon occurrence; when a senior member of a gang was caught and going before the judge for sentencing, the other gang members would show up and sit in the back of the room, perhaps for emotional support for the gang leader or maybe to attempt to intimidate the judge.

He looked at the docket, and sure enough, one of the kids coming up for sentencing with one of the other probation officers was a known gang leader.

He turned around again to look at the group and realized that the younger brother, who had just shown up on his caseload, was right there in the middle of the other gang members. This was all happening on a school day, in the middle of the day, when the kid should have been in school.

Recalling what his boss told him about the principal's recommendation, my brother decided he was going to make sure the kid knew that he needed to get back to school.

My brother watched for an opportunity, and after about ten minutes, the younger brother got up and went into the hallway, presumably to go to the bathroom. There was still some time before my brother was to be up in front of the judge, so he followed the kid into the hallway. At first he couldn't find him, so he headed for the men's room, and just as my brother was entering, the boy was exiting.

Now, my brother's a pretty big, intimidating guy, 6'2", tattoos, etc. Let's just say he knows how to get people's attention.

Without physically touching him, he pointed his finger toward the kid's chest and just read him the riot act: "What the heck are you doing? Why aren't you in school? You're sitting here in the back of the courtroom showing support for your gang buddies? You want me to take you in front of that judge right now, and you want to explain to him why you're not in school? He'll sentence you right here. You want me to do that?"

The kid was backed up against the wall, his eyes as big as saucers. Finally my brother paused and asked, "What do you have to say for yourself?"

The boy looked at him and said, "Um, sir, I'm actually here with my class on a field trip."

Oops!

When my brother returned to the courtroom, he looked again and realized that the group wasn't entirely made up of gang members. It was indeed a class on a field trip. The teacher was sitting in the middle of the group, but she was rather young and my brother didn't recognize her as the teacher.

Reflecting after the fact, my brother realized that he had immediately gone with his erroneous beliefs and jumped all the way to the faulty conclusion that the boy was there as a gang member, supporting the senior gang leader being sentenced. And more than that, my brother actually took action on that wrong conclusion. He didn't actively search for data that could have proved his original hypothesis false. As a result, he had to backpedal a little bit.

Now, in fairness to my brother, the upside is that he did make an impression on the kid. My brother got a call the next day from the kid's mother, who told him, "I don't know what you said to my son, but whatever it was, keep it up. He said he's never skipping school again."

It had a happy ending, but at the same time, it was a lesson learned to not rely solely on your own beliefs but to actually question them before you go into action.

• •

Bias #5: Gambler's bias. This bias is actually comprised of several related biases. It's about believing that: (a) since an event hasn't occurred for some time, it probably won't happen anytime soon; (b) since it has occurred recently, it won't repeat anytime soon; (c) since it has occurred recently, it is now more likely to occur again; or (d) since it hasn't occurred recently, it's due!

If I roll a seven on the dice three times in a row and think I need to get to the casino because I'm on a streak, I'm indulging in gambler's bias, or gambler's fallacy. Just because I'm rolling sevens doesn't mean I'm going to continue to do so. There's no empirical evidence to say it's more likely or less likely that I'm going to get a seven after I roll sevens three times in a row. All things being equal, whether or not you roll a seven is based purely on statistical probabilities.

Here's another example. There are certain areas of California that are more earthquake prone than others. That's a fact. Historical data shows that the area around the San Andreas Fault is especially vulnerable. But if you went through a big earthquake like we had in Santa Barbara in 1978 and then said, "Well, we survived that one. Now we won't have another one for at least fifteen years," then you would be succumbing to the gambler's fallacy.

History has shown that aftershocks are common, some quakes are precursors to bigger ones, etc. There's no statistical evaluation you can make to justify a belief that having one earthquake will or won't lead to another. It's simply not accurate to gauge the probability of a future earthquake solely on your past experience.

Think about auto repair. If you take your car in for a major repair, it would be tempting to believe that the car will be good for another five years before it needs another major repair, right? What evidence do you have to support that? Conversely, you may think that the $2,000 repair you just had done signals another one is on the way; the car is getting old, it's time to get a new one. Yet, realistically, the car could go another hundred thousand miles before another major repair. You just don't know. You're basing your opinion on interpreting the past in order to predict the future. That's where we fall victim to gambler's bias.

Many events are purely random, even though some appear to have patterns. To get confirmation, you must look at the data skeptically and be aware of your own biases.

Bias #6: Overreliance on personal experience. This bias is about not recognizing the limits of your own knowledge or experience; it's believing that your own personal experience is more valid than other data.

For example, in my speaking engagements, I will often ask participants to determine if there are more words in the English language that start with the letter K or more words that have the letter K as the third letter. After quickly running through their memory banks, the vast majority of people say that there are more words that start with a K than those that have K as the third letter. They're basing their conclusion on personal experience: "Hmm, words that start with K: kangaroo, kayak, kazoo, knowledge, knock. But the only word I can think of with a K as the third letter is 'awkward.' So it must be that more words start with K than have K as a third letter," they might reason.

That's personal experience. It's going with a very limited subset, very limited research, and then definitively declaring the answer.

In this example, the reality is that the opposite is true. More words have K as the third letter than start with K. You'd simply have to do a little research to find this out.

This can be a dangerous—or expensive—bias to have and one that I'm guilty of myself. For many years, I've been chairman of the board at the preschool my children attended. The school didn't have a computer lab, and I believed we needed one. "These preschoolers are never going to be at a time in their lives when they won't be using a computer," I said, pushing for the space to put in the computer lab. It was a big effort on my part—I got the computers donated, got everything set up and networked, and so on.

Then I challenged each of the teachers to incorporate the computers into their curriculum. This was going to be huge for preschool kids to learn computers, I thought.

A couple of years later, the director called me at the beginning of the school year and said, "We need to get rid of the computer lab." No, I replied, the children need it! So she told me to come and watch the kids work and it would all make sense to me.

All right, I thought, I'll humor her. But I knew those kids needed a computer lab. If the teachers were having challenges incorporating the computers into their teaching plan, well, that was a fixable problem, and not a good reason to get rid of the lab.

I walked in, and she said, "Watch the kids." The teacher brought in a new group of preschoolers and told them that they were going to use computers today.

Each preschooler found a seat in front of the computer, and the first thing they all did was reach up and start poking at the screen with their fingers. The problem? These computers were equipped with a keyboard and mouse, not a touchscreen.

When the teacher tried to explain to the kids how to use the machines, they were all baffled. Then she handed each an iPad and they immediately went to work without hesitation.

So we got rid of the computer lab and replaced it with a bunch of iPads.

My own personal experience was that a computer lab meant personal computers, keyboards, and mice. But kids today have been raised on touchscreen technology. They are true digital natives. I didn't have that in my experience; therefore, I only knew my way of doing things, which wasn't the only way or even the best way.

Bias #7: Ignoring the losing proposition. Also known as "entrapment," this bias is a bit like the wishful thinking bias, just on steroids. With this bias, you feel that you have to continue to invest time, energy, money, and resources because you've already invested so much time, energy, money, and resources into whatever the decision is. You keep going because you just know it's got to pay off at some point.

I spent many years in the automotive diagnostics industry. One of the service stations I was working with wanted to increase revenue and improve customer satisfaction. So they added three more hours at the end of the workday, from 5:00 to 8:00 at night, because the owners of the service station believed that customers would bring their cars in after work.

The company invested a truckload of time, resources, and energy coming up with a plan for that extended work schedule. Yet after about three years, only about fifty customers in total had used the service. To keep going that long in spite of the evidence that the idea wasn't meeting a need, and solely because of the significant start-up investment, was entrapment.

This bias happens in the stock market all the time. Sometimes people throw so much money at a stock that they think they've got to hang onto it until it bounces back, when in reality it may never bounce back. If you were to look at that same stock today and examine its performance and the company's fundamentals, would you invest in it? Your answer should help you determine if you're suffering from this bias of ignoring the losing proposition.

Entrapment makes you feel like you're stuck in something because you've already invested so much into it. The attachment to the situation is emotional; you don't want to evaluate it, because if you did, you'd realize that you'd be better off getting out.

Bias #8: The insufficient sample size. This bias is a little like the overreliance on personal belief bias, except that this one is based on data. The problem with this bias is that the data relied on is insufficient to arrive at the conclusions due to the relatively small sample size.

One example of this was a Global Leadership and Organizational Behavior Effectiveness (GLOBE) study that came out some years ago. It was a massive, ten-year study of culture involving over seventeen thousand participants and nearly two hundred different scholars. The study took the data, extrapolated it, and concluded that there are nine behavioral tendencies that will differ depending on your cultural background. Since there were over seventeen thousand participants, it was a decidedly significant study, larger than any done before.

But in reality, one could argue that seventeen thousand people out of a world population of around seven billion is a really insignificant sample size (representing less than .0003 percent). Obviously, no one would take the results of this study and decide that everyone of a certain culture behaves a certain way. And the GLOBE study acknowledged this caution and recognized that, while generalizations can be made, given the size of the study, exceptions are to be expected.

For example, one senior-level executive in the study—who didn't own a passport and had never traveled outside a fifty-mile radius of his hometown—had a hard time wrapping his mind around a statistic that said one in five people in the world is Chinese. He couldn't believe it was true, because he knew thousands of people and only a handful of them were Chinese.

Statistically speaking, approximately one person in five worldwide is Chinese (about 1.4 billion out of a total global population of 7.4 billion, or 19%). But the executive's sample size was comparatively very small, so that was his frame. Very few of the people in his network of thousands were Chinese, so therefore that statistic could not be true, he reasoned.

That is an insufficient sample size (not to mention an over-reliance on personal experience). But we tend to base a lot of decisions on the limited experience that we have.

This is an especially relevant bias today when you consider that people base so many of their decisions on something they read online or on the latest trend. Mehmet Oz (Dr. Oz) is a smart man, but you should verify whether his advice is best; even he will tell you that. If you don't verify, then you're at risk of falling victim to the bias of an insufficient sample size. Do your research. Get a second (or third) opinion. Look for doctors that disagree with Dr. Oz's advice (thus fighting confirmation bias). Nowadays there's really no excuse to blindly trust an insufficient sample size.

Bias #9: Focus blindness. This bias is about being so focused on one piece of the problem that you miss other pieces of it.

In some of my workshops, I use the famous "gorilla experiment," a classic video of some people bouncing a basketball. I instruct my group to count the number of times that the people in the video pass the ball to each other. You need to pay attention, I tell the group, because the people are moving in a circle, there are two basketballs, and every pass counts. Don't count the dribbles, just the passes.

Then I show the video, and there's music playing in the background. The people in my workshop group focus intently and count the passes; there are two balls moving through the air and being bounce-passed between about eight people, all of whom are rotating in a circle at the same time.

In the middle of all this activity, a person dressed in a gorilla suit walks across the scene behind the people passing the balls; he walks into the frame from one side, stops in the middle of the frame and beats his chest, then walks out of the frame on the other side.

After the video plays, I ask the group for their count of the passes, and I get the whole gamut of numbers. Then I ask if they noticed anything strange about the video. Amazingly, about half of the people didn't see the gorilla, because they were so focused on counting the passes. This exercise has been done live, and it's been done with other animal characters, all with similar results.

This is a prime example of what I call focus blindness; it's focusing so much on a particular element that you unintentionally miss the surrounding data. This is a bias because you're not even aware that you're missing the data.

When you're in a decision-making situation, it's important to step back enough to see all the data instead of focusing only on the smaller pieces.

The second time I show the video, I tell people to look for the gorilla, and everyone sees it. Just by specifying the focus, or by phrasing instructions or questions in a certain way, the people in the group are pointed toward the "correct" answer.

. . . .

MATH EXERCISE

One of the exercises in my workshops is a math problem, where a man drives his car from point A to point B, continues to point C, and finally arrives at point D, all without stopping. The distance between the points, and the man's rate of speed, are different depending on the section of the trip. All necessary information is provided, and there is no trick. The goal is to figure out how much time it takes the man to make the complete journey without stopping.

As part of the exercise, I pass out cards on which is written almost thirty different pieces of information—questions or statements of fact, only a handful of which actually matter (but the participants don't know this). Among the information provided are unfamiliar words for various units of measure such as "wutts," "dops," and "lors." These are completely ambiguous terms that don't mean anything in English. Of course, I also provide the way to convert the unfamiliar units, albeit through several calculations, into units that are more familiar, such as miles, hours, etc.

The process most groups in my workshops go with is that they immediately convert the unfamiliar units to miles, miles per hour, etc. and then calculate how many hours it takes to travel the distance. They go through this massive set of calculations with distances, times, rates of speed, etc. in order to get the answer in terms of hours, when all they really need to do is tell me how many lors it takes. One of the cards even states that lors is a measure of time, but no one is comfortable using lors as a measure of time on its own. Instead, they try to force the solution into hours, a measure they're more comfortable with. Their own bias toward units with which they are familiar and away from units that make them uncomfortable causes them to perform numerous unnecessary calculations, complicating the problem tremendously, and dragging down their efficiency in solving the problem.

Now, when I give this exercise to kids—for example, a group of fifth-graders—they get it right in no time at all. They have no problem thinking in terms of lors. They don't need to force lors into familiar terms, because, on average, they're experiencing somewhere between twenty and thirty new words every single day anyway. So what's a few more unfamiliar terms? No problem! They haven't yet established biases toward familiar terms as deep as the adults.

There's a great bumper sticker that reads: "The only difference between a rut and a grave is its depth." If you're in a rut, stop digging. If a piece of data doesn't fit your framework, focus on it. Think about it. It may help you get out of your rut.

. . . .

CONCLUSION

In dealing with your own internal biases, it's important to actively seek out people, data, and information that run contrary to your beliefs. It's about looking for other perspectives, not necessarily just relying on the data that you already have or the data you are comfortable with.

This brings up another bias where data is concerned; it's natural to want to focus only on what is measurable. But some things simply aren't measurable. That means that sometimes you may need to consider your gut feelings while checking as much as possible for various viewpoints from other people, especially those who think differently than you. It's not that your gut is wrong—it's that you need to get other opinions to validate or to poke holes in your beliefs.

Henry Ford had a great quote: "If I had asked people what they wanted, they would have said 'faster horses.'" Instead, he focused on the automobile. So don't throw out your beliefs just because other people believe differently—but when you're heavily outweighed, you should carefully examine why you believe your perspective or conclusion is accurate.

Emotions can be a big factor in poor decision making. Studies have shown that people make poorer decisions when they're stressed. If you sense that you are under stress, that you are being rushed, or that you have a strong emotional reaction toward a situation, your ability to think rationally will likely be limited and you may fall more easily into one or more of the biases that I've just discussed. There is a proven physiological reaction happening in your central nervous system when you are under stress, and it's not conducive to making the best decision possible. If you know you've got a strong emotion or reaction to a particular piece of information or a situation, that's the trigger to get other people involved and to be on high alert for your own biases.

Making good decisions starts with being aware of your own biases. Then you must seek different perspectives and then weigh those different opinions and viewpoints against your own. Don't just immediately dismiss someone else's input as ignorance; give it adequate weight and be open to the idea that the other person may actually have a valid point.

The biases discussed in this chapter are sometimes the hardest to recognize because they are internal, and often they only become external when they are formulated into an argument. In the next chapter, we'll talk about recognizing false arguments in others and in ourselves. These arguments tend to be more verbal in nature and hence a bit easier to recognize.

TAKEAWAYS

1. Take a few minutes to think about your own internal biases. In reading this chapter, which biases felt the most familiar?

2. What happened recently that exposed one of your internal biases?

3. In your past, can you think of decisions
    that have been negatively impacted by your
    internal biases?

4. Recognizing that bias now, what can you
    do differently moving forward to become
    aware of that bias in real time? What are
    the triggers? What are the warning signs?

Visit the Institute for the Advancement of Critical
Thinking, www.theiact.org, for more information on
biases and common errors in thinking.

CHAPTER 3

COMMON PATTERNS OF WEAK ARGUMENTS

I n the previous chapter, we looked at biases or fallacies in our own internal logic. Now let's shift our focus and look at the most-common patterns of weak arguments of others that are often recognizable when a verbal discussion or argument arises.

The most important baseline skills in recognizing these patterns is to learn how to listen critically to the arguments of others and identify where the logic—or the applicability of their argument to the current situation—falls apart. These are the key skills necessary to outsmart VUCA.

It's important to recognize these common patterns so that you can keep from being persuaded by them and can instead get at the truth. Some arguments based on these patterns are very persuasive, and if you don't recognize them as being erroneous, as the weak arguments they really are, then they can actually be quite powerful . . . and dangerous!

At the same time, if you understand these patterns, it's possible to use them to sway a conversation—but you must not deliberately use them for your own gain at the expense of the other person. Knowing how they work does not give you the ethical permission to use them to cloud an issue or to persuade somebody who, if they knew the truth about the situation, would decide differently. Notwithstanding attorneys who are schooled in these techniques and use them to do their jobs, using these patterns to manipulate an outcome could create a less-than-ideal outcome for all parties involved. In the wise words of Spiderman's uncle, "With great power comes great responsibility!"

It's crucial to understand these patterns to ensure they are not being used in your business negotiations and discussions, internally or externally. Many of these common patterns are meant to trigger emotions, kick your amygdala into high gear, get adrenaline coursing through your veins, and get you to react rather than to think through the situation, cognitively utilizing your frontal lobes. When we're under the influence of a strong emotion, either positive or negative, the thinking part of our brain checks out, and it becomes difficult to exert control over our behavior. That's when the fight-or-flight mechanism takes over, which frankly should not be in charge when you're trying to make a critical decision.

When you recognize this happening in a business situation—whether within yourself or in someone else—you need to keep your own emotions in check in order to manage the situation rationally.

Being swept away with emotion is not always a bad thing. It's okay to get caught up in the excitement of a motivational speaker, for example. But do it cognitively—recognize that you're enthralled by the words of a powerful orator. I'm not advocating that everyone turn into Mr. Spock from *Star Trek* or Sheldon from *The Big Bang Theory* (depending on your generation), where you're not swayed by emotion and you're all about pure logic with no filters. The goal here is to be aware when people are trying to get an emotional reaction from you. If you choose to go along, fine, as long as you are making a conscious choice.

As a business leader, it's important to recognize these common patterns when they're being used by someone in your organization so that you can keep that person from biasing or swaying the entire team.

Thankfully, many of us who have children are pretty good at recognizing these patterns; school-age kids use them pretty blatantly. "If you *really* loved me, you'd get me that cellphone," your teen might whine. Give me a break; I can see right through that. But the patterns get much more nuanced and subtle as the kids get older, and once they enter the business world, these patterns become harder to detect. "If you really valued our partnership, you would give in on this issue." It's the same flawed argument, but in a business setting we don't recognize it for what it is.

There are a lot of reasons people use these common patterns of weak arguments. On the surface, it may seem like it's the desire to win at all costs or to maintain a relationship. But in reality, there's often an ulterior motive such as prestige or power.

There are financial and strategic reasons for recognizing weak arguments in a business setting, especially arguments that take advantage of our emotions. For instance, there are many examples of products that were introduced based on the emotional involvement of the executive overseeing that product. Launching a product based on emotion—believing in the promise of riches without any market research—is using the wrong argument to make a decision. Without recognizing the characteristics that define these weak arguments, a company stands to lose a lot of money and market share and may even go out of business entirely.

On a personal level, recognizing these weak arguments can keep you from being manipulated and also allows you to make better decisions in every aspect of your life, from negotiations for a new car to getting your kids to do their chores.

So, with that said, here are some common patterns that indicate a weak argument.

Pattern #1: The slippery slope. This pattern is about painting such a dire picture—either step by step or with an illogical conclusion—that the other person will agree to just about anything. It usually follows this formula: If A happens, then before you know it B, C, and D will happen, and that will ultimately lead to E, which would be a disaster. It's about trying to motivate the other person by playing on their emotions, by creating the impression that "the sky is falling." The sky isn't really falling, but if someone creates a worst-case scenario that appears to be inevitable if we start with step A, then others are often more than willing to go along.

It's the old metaphor about allowing the camel to stick its nose in the tent: Don't do it, or pretty soon you'll have the entire camel in the tent. If an action gets started, then a negative end is imminent. That's not necessarily so, because a lot of things can happen between steps A and E—we could take a different path or we could pull the plug on the whole idea. The person using the slippery slope pattern may make an argument that sounds completely logical, but in reality it's one of many possible paths and many options. It's called a slippery slope because the thinking is that, once you step on the slope, there's no other option than to go all the way to the bottom. Usually, that's just not the case.

I heard a local politician here in California recently talking about a proposal to get stricter sanitation grades for restaurants because there were some minor issues at one or two local restaurants. The politician's position was against the stricter grades and in favor of the restaurants, saying that stricter sanitation grades for restaurants are unnecessary and would force many of the restaurants to close their doors, costing hundreds of jobs, because of the increased costs associated with this "needless" regulation. Slippery slope! But again, in reality there are a lot of steps in between passing the new requirements and hundreds of people losing their jobs where things could go differently. True, if we have stricter sanitation grades, restaurants may have to spend some money to comply. If they have to spend money, they may have to charge more. But if every restaurant has to spend more, and then raise their rates to recoup those expenses, then it stands to reason that each individual restaurant won't be at a competitive disadvantage and won't have to shut down.

Another example I heard recently was an argument in favor of keeping the death penalty. This is a hot-button issue—one of those emotionally charged topics—where you'll often find a slippery slope. The argument was that getting rid of the death penalty would allow criminals free rein and no one would be safe.

Now, there are a lot of steps between getting rid of the death penalty and criminals having free rein. There are a lot of assumptions in this argument, hence it should not be accepted at face value.

And yet the thought of no one being safe, of criminals running freely in the streets, is such an emotional trigger for many that they'll agree that yes, we must keep the death penalty.

The key to evaluating any weak argument is to hit the pause button, go back to step one, and evaluate the individual points of the equation before jumping to the end result.

Remember, however, that people often don't like to have their arguments picked apart. To do so may earn you the label of someone who supports the opposing view—even though all you're doing is pointing out the errors, or the slippery slope pattern, of the argument at hand. Recognizing the common pattern is one thing. What you do with that recognition is an entirely different decision!

The slippery slope doesn't always play on fear, ending with a negative result. It can be used for aspirational goals as well. For example, by buying a lottery ticket, just think what you could do with those millions! You could buy your own island and retire tomorrow. Well, first you've got to buy a ticket, then it's got to win, then it's got to be a significant amount, and so on.

The slippery slope is dangerous in a business setting, particularly if you have an executive making very bad, emotional decisions because he or she is only looking at the most positive or the most negative possible outcome and not looking at the relevant data, seeking other points of view, and weighing the decisions carefully and without bias. People in business often use the slippery slope to argue that the company must expand or die (negative) or that an acquisition will allow the company to dominate the market (positive).

Pattern #2: The bandwagon. This pattern is about wanting to be like everyone else, a desire not to be left behind. In fact, a relatively new term entering the common lexicon is FOMO, or the Fear of Missing Out, defined as the "anxiety that an exciting or interesting event may currently be happening elsewhere." Everyone's doing it, so I have to also. I just read a letter to the editor that said, "If you're serious about business, you use an Android phone." I'm serious about business, so does that mean I should get an Android? Well, there goes my Blackberry!

The bandwagon is about following along because the illusion has been created that everyone in the group that I aspire to be a part of does certain things or that they do things a certain way. It's up to you to vet the validity of the claims. What are they doing, and why are they doing it? There are a lot of fallacies in the bandwagon logic that you need to examine before just accepting it at face value. What they say may be true, but by the same token, there are innumerable ways that going along with others could end up badly for you. Remember being a teenager?

In business, it's very tempting to be drawn in by the bandwagon pattern. If your competitors are all spending money on research and development right now, it might be tempting to believe that you need to also. But first consider why they are all spending. Maybe it's because they're playing catch-up to your company. You must examine all the facts before going with a knee-jerk reaction based on what everyone else is doing.

In an argument or a negotiation, if you don't recognize that someone is using the bandwagon pattern, then you may come to the wrong conclusion; you may want to jump right in and say, "We've got to have that, too." But you need to pause and examine the argument to see if someone is trying to coerce you into a certain course of action. If someone tries to use the bandwagon pattern in their discussion with you, they're trying to play on your inherent FOMO or even your fear of being ridiculed for being different.

It's human nature to want to be part of the "successful" group, part of the "in" crowd, whatever the situation. On some level, it's part of a survival instinct; people who belonged to a strong tribe lived longer lives than those who went it alone. That desire to belong begins when we're young, and it continues to be felt into adulthood and in the working world, where it gets a little more dangerous—financially, legally, and so on.

One final note on this pattern. The advertising industry has used the bandwagon pattern for many years, to the point where it has begun to lose its effectiveness, thus forcing ad agencies to be a bit more subtle with the pattern. It's still being used, but now through social media, organized flash mobs, judiciously used hashtags, viral videos, opportunistic product placement, and so on. You've got to evaluate information independently and with a clear and rational mind.

Pattern #3: The false dichotomy. According to the logic of the false dichotomy, you only have two choices, A or B. There is no middle ground. There are no other alternatives.

For example, if we don't outlaw all cars, we will destroy the Earth. The logic goes like this: Cars produce pollution; pollution pokes holes in the ozone layer; without the ozone layer, we're all going to die; game over. Oh, and by the way, if you're not with us, you're against us. If you're not part of the solution, you're part of the problem.

The false dichotomy is polarizing; it eliminates any compromise. If you're not north, you're south; if it's not black, it's white; if you're not hot, you're cold. There's no equator, no gray, no lukewarm. There is no moderate position.

With the false dichotomy, one side of the argument is so abhorrent that it causes an emotional reaction that makes us automatically take the other side. *Well, I don't want to die, so we've got to get rid of cars,* you may think, as the answer to the ozone problem. But isn't there another way to save us all? What about electric cars or hybrids?

The person using false dichotomy is trying to promote one conclusion by suggesting extreme consequences of the other solution or other course of action. It's not meant to get at the truth, it's meant to push you in a certain direction that the person who is arguing wants you to go. Many philosophers, religious leaders, and rulers of civilizations throughout history have used this pattern to influence people and, in some tragic cases, to manipulate their followers.

In business, the false dichotomy is used to force someone into a decision. If you are weighing evidence and there are good arguments on both sides, and then someone jumps in with an argument that suddenly makes you feel pushed one way or the other, you must hit the pause button. Ask whether the argument is valid or if actually there's a middle ground and you're just being pressured by the impression of a dichotomy that really doesn't exist.

Pattern #4: The red herring. This is a well known, and often practiced, diversionary pattern meant to distract from the key issue. People use this pattern when they cannot (or choose not to) address the issue at hand.

For example, a number of years back in a coastal city near my hometown of Santa Barbara, the ocean's pollution levels made the seafood unsafe to eat. We were all warned not to eat shellfish and other seafood from the local waters. Then a politician came out stating that we needed to think about the poor fishermen, the people who relied on selling fish for a living. How were they going to feed their families? How were they going to stay in business?

He was trying to cloud the issue by playing on peoples' sympathies—eat seafood so that we don't send the fishermen and their families into poverty.

While the other patterns we've talked about so far are based on false issues or at best have a kernel of truth, the red herring uses a real issue that is not directly related to the topic at hand to confuse the discussion. In the fish example, the topic at hand is the safety of eating fish because of the levels of toxins. The diversionary pattern is: How are people that fish for a living going to feed their families? The red herring (the faulty argument, not the fish) is meant to get you to focus on something other than the issue you're wrestling with.

Politicians use the red herring pattern often. When they get asked a very difficult question, they reframe the question in a way that sounds like it's related, but it's really not. The way they'll rephrase the question makes people think they came up with a great answer, but in reality, their answer has essentially nothing to do with what was originally asked. And if the reporter who asked the original question points out this pattern in their follow-up question, he or she is often not invited back to the next press conference.

Sometimes the red herring is used when the decision-making process is already distracted; it's almost like a magic trick—ignore what I'm doing with my right hand and focus on my left hand instead. The red herring is about shifting the focus away from where you really ought to be looking and getting you to focus instead on the diversion.

Pattern #5: Chicken-and-egg reasoning. Sometimes known as circular reasoning, this is an argument that restates the conclusion rather than actually proving the conclusion. An example of this was a comment I heard not too long ago. Someone said: "Colin Powell is an incredible communicator because he speaks so well." Well, you could also say, "Colin Powell speaks so well because he's such a great communicator."

That's chicken-and-egg, or circular reasoning; the two parts of the statement mean essentially the same thing, one part of the statement just reinforces the other. In other words, as an answer to a question, the person refers back to the argument he just made.

Often this pattern is used when there's no solid argument, so the person using it tries to employ different wording. He'll use different phrases, different ways of saying the exact same thing. When you really peel the onion, you'll find an argument like, "Math is exact because it's precise." That's not an argument; it's not persuasive. "Exact" and "precise" mean essentially the same thing. You could reverse the order of wording and it would say the same thing. It's a chicken-and-egg, egg-and-chicken thing.

In the business world, this pattern can immediately draw you into an argument; its power lies in affirming a belief you already have. The person presenting the argument knows you believe a certain way and leverages that belief to convince you to go along with their overall argument toward their desired outcome.

As with the other patterns, the conclusion with a chicken-and-egg or circular reasoning argument can't be proven at all.

Trying to prove an argument by restating it as if it were a conclusion doesn't make it so.

Pattern #6: Ad hoc reasoning. This is the attempt to persuade at any cost. Most often, additional arguments will be introduced that only tangentially relate to the topic being argued. It's akin to moving the goalposts after the ball is kicked. Often the argument that is added cannot be proved or disproved.

Let me give you an example. Many years ago, in a former life, I went to a seminar touting ESP—extrasensory perception. The speaker announced that he was going to prove that ESP existed: "As long as everybody in the auditorium believes that ESP is possible, I will be able to prove it exists beyond the shadow of a doubt. If everyone believes, then I will be able to read your thoughts," he said.

By his logic, only if everyone present believed in ESP would he be able to read minds in the room. But if he couldn't read anyone's mind, it wouldn't be because ESP didn't exist; it would be because someone in the room didn't believe in it. With this logic, there would never be a way to prove that ESP did not exist. That's ad hoc reasoning.

In business, people throw anything and everything into an argument—they'll even use the absence of evidence to make an argument. And the way their arguments are often set up, they can never be proved false. Anything that's said that might prove the argument false is effectively marginalized under a belief system that is so amorphous that you can't put your arms around it.

In the end, the person using ad hoc reasoning is often just employing a lot of rhetoric to try to get his or her way.

This is where the Socratic method really helps. When someone tries to use ad hoc reasoning with you, ask questions. Ask lots of questions. Just keep asking questions until you get to the root of the argument. When you reach the "because I said so" of the argument, you know you have arrived.

The Socratic method was largely created to combat the ad hoc reasoning that was going on during the time of Socrates. People were making assertions without backing them up. They were in positions of authority (which is the other place you often see ad hoc reasoning). Authority figures often get away with ad hoc reasoning because people just trust that what they're saying is true. But if enough questions are posed, often it's discovered that the argument is based in faith and belief, not facts and rational thought. Indeed, the emperor truly has no clothes!

Pattern #7: Ad hominem. This common pattern involves rejecting a proposal or conclusion based on where it comes from. *Ad hominem* is Latin for "to the man," so the ad hominem pattern is about attacking the arguer, not the argument.

This happens in politics and business all the time. Someone decides not to buy Microsoft Office, because Microsoft is trying to create a monopoly. It's not about buying the best product, it's about taking a stand against a corporation.

Or take religion, for another example. Some might say a reverend is a fundamentalist, so his objections to evolution can't be taken seriously. That's not evaluating whether his argument has value; it's throwing his argument out because of who he is. Ad hominem is saying the CEO of *x* company got caught cheating on his taxes, therefore the quality of the company's products can't be trusted either.

Ad hominem is also related to first impressions. It's very tempting to judge a person based on their appearance without giving them the benefit of the doubt. If someone comes into a meeting dressed sloppily, or with messy hair, or wearing a stained shirt, then people may dismiss their input based solely on appearance. Often we do this subconsciously. Again, it's human nature.

It's also done consciously by salespeople to cloud an issue. For example, I recently went in to buy a minivan with my wife. The Honda car salesman tried to steer us away from buying a Toyota Sienna by mentioning that Toyota just had a massive recall. But Toyota didn't have a recall on Siennas—it had a recall on Camrys. The Sienna actually won all kinds of awards. Still, since the salesman wanted us to buy a new Honda Odyssey, one of his products, the Toyota recall was the argument he used. Indeed, when I pointed out this pattern in his argument, he "reasoned" that if one Toyota product is being recalled, then all the company's products have quality issues, and it's just a matter of time before all of them are recalled. (Did you also recognize the slippery slope here?)

Similarly, ad hominem involves disregarding an argument based on something completely unrelated.

In speaking all over the world, I fly quite often, and I remember one flight out of Santa Barbara where a casually dressed older gentleman, probably in his eighties, sat next to me. I was dressed in a suit and, feeling a bit antisocial, I buried my nose in a book in an effort to avoid having a conversation with my elderly neighbor. But he struck up a conversation with me anyway, which I initially hoped to bring to an expeditious close.

Soon enough, he asked me what I do for a living, and I decided I would impress him with all my credentials, my degrees, and my experience in speaking and working all over the world. I figured that would be the end of it, but he kept the conversation going. So, assuming by his appearance that he was long retired, I asked him, "What did you do when you were working?"

He told me he was still working. In fact, he worked at the University of California in Santa Barbara (UCSB) in the physics department. Since I graduated from UCSB, I started to get a little interested. I told him my name, and when I asked his, I discovered that he made the news recently by being awarded the Nobel Prize! I was sitting next to a Nobel laureate, but I almost missed out on our conversation because I judged him based on first appearances. We ended up having a wonderful conversation, and I learned a very important lesson that day.

That's the danger of ad hominem. We disregard the discussion brought to the table based on something completely unrelated to the inherent quality of the argument.

Ad hominem makes us vulnerable when others tap into a bias we already have. For example, if you exclude someone's input because of his political or religious persuasion, that's ad hominem. If someone is a Democrat or a Muslim or from Texas (or California or New York or...), and it causes an immediate visceral reaction against whatever it is they are saying, you're dealing with ad hominem.

By the way, ad hominem also comes into play when the trait is seemingly positive—for example, including someone on a team at work just because they graduated from an Ivy League school. Does graduating from a particular school have something to do with what you're asking them to do? If the answer is no, then you're dealing with ad hominem; the situation is playing on your preconceived ideas. The tendency or trait is being ascribed to that person only because of your perception of who they are.

The ad hominem pattern is a sign of a weak argument, where you attack the arguer (or the person, group, company, or organization) rather than dealing with the actual argument or the validity of the facts.

CONCLUSION

These common patterns of weak arguments are used because they have been proven to be persuasive and powerful. People often use these patterns when they know they don't have a solid argument, and they try to cloud the issue in order to get their way. Other people use these patterns out of habit, knowing from experience that they work. They may not even be aware that they're doing it, but they're getting the results that they want, and this reinforces the subconscious decision to use these patterns again and again.

Whether used consciously or subconsciously, these patterns of weak arguments are used because they often work and most people don't immediately recognize them.

Once you learn how to recognize these patterns, make sure that you can put your head on your pillow at night knowing that *you* haven't used any of them in ways that are inconsistent with your own ethical frame.

Our goal is to be able to outsmart VUCA and recognize some of the most common patterns of weak arguments. In the next two chapters, we'll look at specific methodologies to ensure that the argument we're hearing, or the argument we're making, doesn't fall into one of these traps.

TAKEAWAYS

1. Think about the last time you were in a meeting where an argument did not sit right with you. Which of the common patterns discussed in this chapter were being used?

2. The next time you read the news or turn on the television, try to identify one or two common patterns of weak arguments in the material you're seeing.

3. What internal biases do you have that might cause you to "attack the man," to be guilty of the pattern ad hominem?

Visit the Institute for the Advancement of Critical Thinking, www.theiact.org, for more information on common patterns of weak arguments.

CHAPTER 4

OUTSMARTING VUCA SOLO: THE PROCESS FOR ENSURING TOP-QUALITY DECISIONS

Outsmarting VUCA is a methodology—a set of tools and a process that you can use as an individual to make sure you are thinking as critically as you can. Outsmarting VUCA takes effort, so it is useful particularly when you have to make important decisions.

Some decisions obviously don't require a whole lot of thinking: Where will I go for lunch? When am I going to buy gas for the car? These are easy decisions that don't require a lot of thinking.

But when the stakes are high, the risk of failure is substantial, or the outcome is potentially negative or hugely beneficial, you need to spend a little more time practicing the skills required to outsmart VUCA.

If you try to make critical decisions in a random fashion, without tools or a process, you are more likely to make mistakes. You'll tend to go back to your default way of thinking—with its inherent biases and blind spots—which is not ideally suited to rationally considering an important situation or decision. And when operating alone, without access to input from others, it's a challenge to identify and mitigate all of our blind spots. But we can at least learn and follow a process that has been proven to help identify blind spots and to lead to better decision making.

The information in this chapter will help you prepare as an individual for outsmarting VUCA and making good decisions when you don't have the benefit of leveraging a team of people that could add value to the decision-making process. Consider this a lesson in "solo" outsmarting VUCA!

THINK DIFFERENTLY

When making a major decision, it's important to look at the situation from various perspectives. Earlier in the book we discussed how different people taking different roles can be beneficial in the decision-making process; one person can take the role of the antagonist, another the role of the protagonist, etc. When making a decision on an individual basis, these roles are all played by you—they represent the various perspectives you need to take in order to examine the situation.

For example, the opportunity to accept a position with a new company that would require a move halfway across the country is a big decision and not one to be taken lightly. As a way of deciding whether to pursue the opportunity, you should go through the process of looking at the situation from various perspectives, really taking on different roles in your head. Many of us do this without even realizing we're doing it. Now perform this task deliberately and methodically in order to examine the issue from several key angles, and you'll begin the process of solo outsmarting VUCA—instead of just packing up the car and taking off for what sounds like greener pastures.

By looking at the situation through the process of solo outsmarting VUCA, you can avoid saying to yourself later, "Well, I should've seen that coming," or "I wish I would've considered this more carefully." When you have those regrets, it's usually a sign that you didn't go through the solo outsmarting VUCA process.

Solo outsmarting VUCA begins with an overarching meta-process, if you will, composed of two steps.

The first step is to create an environment that is free of distractions. You need to be as focused as possible so that you can use parts of your brain that you don't typically use on a daily basis. Without this distraction-free environment, it's very easy to fall right back into your regular way of thinking, which hamstrings the entire process.

So start by finding (or creating) a space that allows you to be focused and free of distractions and also a little creative or innovative (in other words, it shouldn't be a stifling or sterile environment). I recommend also having a few simple toys to tinker with—like a Koosh ball or a bunch of pipe cleaners—because these have been shown to stimulate areas of the brain that most people have difficulty tapping into by just sitting and thinking.

Also ensure that your environment has whatever resources you need to help you with the process. You'll need something to use in capturing your ideas, and you'll likely need access to sources of information. So you'll probably need a computer, laptop, or tablet with Internet access. But be forewarned, irrelevant distraction is the enemy of solo outsmarting VUCA (*relevant* distractions, on the other hand, can be quite useful; the key is in knowing the difference).

The second step is to set a deadline. The overall decision-making process needs some sort of timeline to bring it to an end. A constraint on time will force you to think in creative and innovative ways. According to John Kotter in his book *A Sense of Urgency*, this self-imposed time constraint has been shown to be a critical element in driving change, including changing the way you think.

Let me demonstrate. Recently I facilitated a strategic planning retreat for a large manufacturing company. The session was held off-site in a conference center room with no windows and lots of whiteboards. The attendees were the leaders of the company, and their primary focus, the goal established by the CEO, was to improve the company's process time by 10 percent. Many of the executives and leaders in the room thought they could achieve half a percent, or perhaps even 1 percent, but there was simply no way they could reach the goal of 10 percent. For hours they brainstormed and argued but couldn't seem to find a way to get to the goal. They needed to change their thinking. To do that, I needed to stimulate different areas of their brains to outsmart VUCA. By asking one simple question, I was able to shock their thinking in a way that led to a breakthrough. I asked, "What would you need to do in order to shorten your process time by 50 percent?" At first, they threw up their hands in disbelief, stating the very idea was ludicrous; there was simply no way to get there from where they were; they'd have to dynamite everything and start over. But that idea actually stuck: Why can't we dynamite everything, or at least some things, and start over? Can we do that? Is that against the rules? Finally, they started looking at the situation from a radically different perspective.

The point of the exercise was to get them to question their own constraints, and I did that by positing a question that couldn't be answered with their current way of thinking. There was no linear way to get there.

That's the key to this process. You've got to be able to challenge yourself to think in ways that you don't normally think. As Albert Einstein said, "No problem can be solved by the same kind of thinking that created it." You've got to think differently, and that begins by setting up the environment so that you have the ability and the capability to think differently. If you normally work in an office, don't do this exercise in your office, do it somewhere else where you can focus and be free of distraction and constraints.

TAKING ON ROLES

In our natural state, we all tend to think a certain way and tend toward a certain role. For example, if you watch any of the sitcoms or shows on television—*Star Trek*, *The Big Bang Theory*, or *Seinfeld*—there is probably a character you resonate with. Many of the media pundits out there have postulated as to why *The Big Bang Theory* is so popular. In part, I believe it's because there are a lot of people out there who identify with one of the characters on the show.

To be successful at the solo outsmarting VUCA process, you must understand the role you tend toward.

The process itself involves taking on different roles. You must sequentially go through the different roles in this process in order to ensure that you're thinking about the situation or decision from each angle individually. Don't switch between the roles quickly. You must take on each specific role deliberately, and consider the situation from that unique perspective for a focused period of time. Remember, this exercise is limited by your blind spots, experience, and background, but the goal is to examine everything that surrounds the situation or decision from a variety of perspectives as completely as possible.

Assuming each role individually may feel a bit forced at first, but with practice it will become second nature—you'll find yourself switching to the individual roles with little or no thought to the process.

The Detective Role. The first role you must assume is the Detective, or the analytical role. In this role, you need to ask: What's the critical information that I need that should play a role in my decision?

Using the moving-for-a-job-opportunity example, those pieces of information might include the cost of living where you're planning to move, the average size of homes, the quality of schools, and information about aspects of personal life that are important to you. Then, on the business side of the situation: How long has the company been around? What has its performance been like? What is the culture like? Do I know anybody there now or anyone who ever worked there? How many lawsuits have been filed against the company? What would my specific responsibilities be? What do I know about the person I'd report to? And so on.

The Detective role is just about identifying the raw information that you would need in order to make a decision. This step needs to be done very analytically. Why? Because confirmation bias often threatens to intervene at this point in the process. We have a tendency in this first role to identify only information that will support the decision we want to make.

Instead, you should focus on what information you would need to have in order to change your mind. Please don't miss this! If you've already identified that you're leaning toward a particular decision, what information or data would refute or cause you to reverse your decision?

So your primary focus at this stage is to identify and gather the information you need and bring it all together. Now you've got a framework for decision making, and you've assimilated the relevant information. You're not yet ready to make the decision, though. You're just getting started.

The Gut Check Role. The data and information collected by the detective then feeds into the next role that you assume, which is a more emotional role, an intuition-based or heart-centered role. I call this role the Gut Check. What do you like about the idea? What do you dislike? What are your feelings, your fears? In this role, you really attempt to tap into your thoughts, feelings, and beliefs rather than just your rational brain. How does your excitement or dread of the situation affect the decision? Write it down, but don't analyze anything just yet. Your goal is just to capture the raw form of the emotions. Let them flow. If you start to analyze too quickly, you stem the flow and end up with an incomplete and falsely weighted image of your gut-level reaction to the situation or decision.

The Naysayer Role. Next, move into the role of Naysayer. This is the "what if" analysis, focusing on finding the faults in the idea. Ask yourself: What could possibly go wrong with this situation? What are the things that have the greatest risk? Where are the potential pitfalls? What could happen that would make this a mistake? What's the probability of these things happening?

> Visit the Institute for the Advancement of Critical Thinking, www.theiact.org for more questions applicable to each role.

Looking at the situation from a negative point of view immediately after looking at it from an emotional angle is a way of balancing out the decision making. You may feel a bit of whiplash at this point, but this is done on purpose. You're forcing your brain to work in ways that it doesn't typically work. Without this "whiplash" of thinking, you can too easily continue with linear thinking that won't let you outsmart VUCA.

The Optimist Role. The next role is the Optimist. This is not a Pollyanna point of view—instead, it's looking at the situation or decision from a logical and optimistic perspective. In other words, what are the benefits of making this decision? What's the upside? What are some possible ways to mitigate the potential pitfalls identified in the Naysayer role?

Now, don't be naïve in this Optimist role. Don't think, *Oh, it'll all work out.* This role is really focused on looking at possible solutions to the problems that were just brought up in the Naysayer role. Think "optimist," not "ostrich." (Don't bury your head in the sand and hope things work out . . . that's not an optimist, that's a flightless bird!) Be solution focused.

RATCHETING UP

The last few roles were like being on a seesaw—first neutral, then emotional, then negative, then positive. No wonder your head hurts!

Now you need to really ratchet up the process.

The Creative Role. The next role you'll step into is the Creative role. What are some other options? How about working virtually? How about doing a trial run and going for three weeks and seeing how it works, but keeping Plan B—to come back home? The stakes are high here, so you need to be creative and innovative about other ways to accomplish the same end result or to minimize the negative aspects and amplify the positive. You may still be able to accomplish what you want but with minimal risk or potential downside.

This role is often the most fun, but it also benefits from putting yourself in a creative and barrier-free environment. Go for a walk. Play with the toys in the room. (You do have some, right?) Doodle. Lie on the floor and look at the room from a different perspective. Stand on a chair. (But don't break any

OSHA rules, please!) Break from your normal way of processing, whatever it takes.

The Organizer Role. Once you've thought through (and written down) all your out-of-the-box ideas, look at where you are from an organizational perspective, stepping into the Organizer role. Are there any gaps in the data? Is any additional information needed? Did the Naysayer bring up any potential pitfalls that the Detective needs to investigate? And so on.

Then iterate. Go back through the roles: be a Detective again and gather more information, step into the emotions of the Gut Check role, think about other downsides of the idea in the Naysayer role, and so on. As you go back through the roles, keep in mind your deadline—don't forget there's a time frame for making this decision. The sense of urgency is key for this solo outsmarting VUCA process to work.

By stepping through these roles, you're forcing yourself to consider the issue from a multitude of angles. The challenge is to force yourself to spend a significant enough period of time on each role. I recommend that you time yourself, because it's too easy to skip over a role. For example, if you're naturally an optimist, you may not spend enough time in the Naysayer role, because your tendency will be to think, *Nothing can possibly go wrong with this idea, the Naysayer role is just a killjoy,* or *I'm sure I've thought of everything in this role.*

A good litmus test for deciding if emotions are negatively impacting a particular role is if, for example, you find yourself essentially negating a role by saying to yourself something like "I'm starting to sound like Fred, and nobody likes Fred. He's always so (fill in the blank)." This is a good indication that the role has triggered something in you that you don't want to look at (and you've just fallen into the ad hominem pattern as well). It's a sign that you need to repeat the process, at least for that role, in a more methodical way. You need to check your emotions at the door to the degree possible. At the very least, you must be aware of your emotions so that you can begin to regulate them so they don't unnecessarily get in the way of outsmarting VUCA.

A FEW RULES AND TIPS

When going through the process, it's important to remain in one role at a time; do not shift between roles during your conversation with yourself. If you're trying to be the Optimist and focus on the benefits, you may feel yourself being sucked into the "yeah, but" mode. That's a different role; keep that role out of the room and remain focused on the optimistic pieces of the discussion, the benefits, the upside.

While this tends to be the most effective flow of roles, you may decide to go through them in a different order, depending on your need. But in my experience with hundreds of companies and thousands of use cases, for most situations the roles tend to flow best in the order I've presented them.

You'll also need some sort of cue when switching from one role to the next. For example, how do you transition from the Detective role to the Gut Check role and reflect on the impact that this decision is having on you? There are two elements required to change in order to signal a transition in your brain.

First, you need to change your body position, for example, stand up and move to a different chair, or if you're inside, move outside. Second, you need to change what you're focusing on visually—if you're writing on paper, switch to the computer screen, if you're looking at your desk, look out the window.

By changing these two elements, your brain recognizes that it's time to change what you're thinking. In a way, it's a bit like character acting. Sometimes I'll even take off a coat or put on a different pair of shoes to help signal to the brain that I'm making that transition. These little tricks have been proven to work, so give them a try.

Transitions tend to be the hardest part of the process. The better you can make those transitions, the more effective this process is going to be.

There are also a series of questions on which each role should focus. Going through that series of questions will also help get you into the mind-set of the next role and help you transition to that role. For example, given the data that I have, what am I feeling about this situation? Am I excited? Afraid? Happy? Sad? And you should plan on customizing the questions as needed to fit the particular situation.

Another tip that many of my clients find useful is to identify from your own experience someone who you would say has a strong propensity toward that particular role. This is what actors do quite often—they think of someone from their past and then imagine how that person would respond to the situation.

People tend to have very strong memories and reactions to certain personalities, people who've had an influential role in their lives. I remember one older gentleman early in my engineering career whose nickname on the team was Eeyore, after the donkey in the *Winnie the Pooh* children's stories. That was his personality; he was a glass-half-empty kind of guy. So when I need to switch into the Naysayer role, I think back to him and say, "How would Eeyore respond to this? Well, he'd probably say, 'This will never work. You didn't think about this, you didn't think about that.'" I don't need to become Eeyore, but I can character act the Naysayer role by thinking about a person from my past and by deliberately and consciously taking on that persona.

This is sometimes an easier way to approach a role than just in the abstract. The more visceral the reaction, the better it's going to allow you to follow this process. Try to think of a character in a cartoon or a movie, a past work associate, or a family member. Family members tend to be great ones to use because we have so much data and so many emotions to tap into in our brains that a purely logical, linear approach won't tap into. What would your mom or dad tell you to do in this situation? Grandma or granddad? Uncle or favorite cousin? Please remember—and this is important—you don't need to agree with them. You're just trying to see the situation from their perspective. They may be wrong, but their input is invaluable in creating a complete picture of the situation or decision.

There are also some physical tools you can use when getting into a role. If you decide to use the character of Spock, for example, print out a picture of him. If the character or person is tangible, when you get ready to take on that role, put that character or person's picture up on the wall.

The key is to find ways to engage and activate the various parts of the brain, especially the ones you don't use that often in your daily work. While pictures stimulate the visual sense, some people find it helpful to stimulate the auditory sense through music. If you're in the Optimist role, play some upbeat music to get your ideas flowing. If corny songs make you happy, play some while you're in that role. Or, if certain scents bring back pleasant memories for you, there are any number of different ways to tap into the olfactory system as well. Take advantage of all five senses any way you can. The process all comes down to your own individual personality and style and finding the best way to completely transition into each role as you go through the solo outsmarting VUCA process.

IN THE WORKPLACE

As an individual, there often isn't enough time to use an extended process like this in the workplace. You may be able to use it, for example, if you need to give a major proposal to your manager or an external customer; instead of walking in unprepared, use this process to really come up with a solid plan.

The better you get at this process, the more balanced and well-reasoned contributions you will be able to make when you are part of a larger group or team. Then you can bring your findings to another person—maybe a subject-matter expert or someone who is naturally glass-half-empty or a creative individual. Get them involved by asking for their input: "What's another way to solve this? What would you recommend?" This way, you can leverage their natural tendencies for one particular role and you don't have to assume all the roles yourself. Think of it as a hybrid solution. Yes, it's not quite solo outsmarting VUCA, but I'm okay bending the rules a bit in the interest of efficiency and efficacy.

As you get better at this process, you'll also get faster at it, and then you'll find it to be useful more often and in more situations.

For example, if a crisis occurs at work and the heat is on, the last thing you'll have is a lot of time for decision making, but you also don't want to end up making a poor decision that may make matters worse.

In a case like this, the first thing you need to do is calm down and get your amygdala under control—get your frontal lobes back in charge. If you make a decision without doing this first, chances are it won't be the best decision because you won't think about it logically, you'll be reacting emotionally. There's a lot of research indicating that you don't want the amygdala in charge when you need to make a high-stakes decision.

Once you've reined in your amygdala, you can go through the decision-making process. It doesn't need to take a copious amount of time, but it does take some practice. I've coached executives for years to where they can now, in the space of about three minutes, go through all of these roles and generate a perspective from each one of them in their brain. In some cases, they even do this exercise on paper, thus strengthening their final decision.

Interestingly, for the roles, I've noticed that in many cases these executives have created amalgams where the image that comes to mind for each role is actually made up of many people who have their core tendency aligned in some way with that particular role. That's when you get good at this process, when the character in the Naysayer role or Optimist role is not composed of a single person but is a combination of people or personas, and it becomes its own living, breathing self. You're in essence creating a character in your head.

Some of the greatest actors are very good at this; you can see on their face when they become the character they've created in their heads. Some of the skills they use are the same skills required for solo outsmarting VUCA. But these skills do take a fair amount of practice before they become second nature.

Once you get good at this process, you'll get a reputation for being levelheaded, unbiased, someone whose emotions are in check and who is able to process things in a logical, rational fashion and come to a brilliant decision.

It's an exciting process when it works. Several of the executives I've coached that are at Fortune 100 companies have attributed a significant portion of their success to getting so good at this process that they now do it without even thinking about it.

Anne Mulcahy was a great practitioner of this at Xerox. She took over Xerox when it was floundering, and by only making the critical decisions up front, and then reserving less time-sensitive decisions until she had more information, she was able to turn around the company. She moved Xerox from losing $273 million in 2000 to earning $859 million in 2004. Xerox's stock rose 75 percent over that time frame, compared with a loss of 6 percent for the Dow Jones Total Stock Market Index.

LIVING WITH YOUR DECISION

The last piece of making a decision using this process is to create a Plan B. This plan should include early warning indicators that you're going to monitor in order to discern whether or not you've made the right decision. Due to the very nature of a

VUCA environment, sometimes our predictions of the future are a bit off, and our decisions need to be reevaluated.

If something appears on your radar that indicates your decision is not the best one, then you need to go through the process again—call on your different roles, make sure that you're not relying solely on emotion, and don't fall into any of the faulty arguments and common patterns of weak arguments that we discussed earlier. Once you know more about the situation, you need to decide if you would make the same decision today given the information that you now have. If the answer is no, then you need to pull the trigger on plan B. By executing plan B now, you're able to succeed by, to paraphrase one of Google's mantras, "failing fast."

Anne Mulcahy of Xerox likened it to a farmer who had a cow stuck in a ditch, according to some advice she received from one of her customers, a Texas farmer. In retelling the story, she says the farmer explained to her that he first had to get the cow safely out of the ditch, then he had to figure out how the cow got into the ditch in the first place, and then he had to make some changes so that the cow would never get stuck in that ditch again.

Sometimes, in spite of the process, our decisions can still derail because in this VUCA environment the decision you made yesterday may not be the best decision tomorrow. When you make a bad decision, step one, get the cow out of the ditch.

Then make a better decision, improve it, limit the damage, and get smarter as you go forward.

Time permitting, another way to check yourself is to use a lifeline and phone-a-friend. Pick up the phone and talk with someone that you know has a mind-set or a perspective that is different than your own, someone who has a different blind spot or who has respectfully challenged you in the past. It must be someone who has your best interests at heart and who is going to steer you in what they believe to be the right direction. Ask this phone-a-friend some key questions: "Here's the situation, what am I missing? What would you recommend here?" See if it aligns. If it doesn't, don't try to rationalize your decision. Instead, uncover why your friend thinks what they think. Your goal is to determine if they see something you don't. You called them for a reason. Assume they are right. Now, what did you miss?

Another way to check yourself is to imagine your decision under public scrutiny. If your decision made the headlines in the newspaper as soon as it was found out, would you be able to stand behind it? Would you be embarrassed by it, do you have a defensible position, or do you feel like you could actually justify it based on your decision criteria?

When you think about the public scrutiny of your decision, if you have a negative gut reaction, that's a red flag. You may need to revisit the process again because something may be missing from your evaluation. The roles capture the most critical perspectives in most decisions or situations, but there may be more going on than these roles can ferret out. Something may be conflicting with your character or your integrity, or there may be something you just can't sleep with; please recognize that this awareness is also part of the solo outsmarting VUCA process.

CONCLUSION

Making pivotal decisions on an individual basis can be difficult. By placing yourself in various roles and asking yourself critical questions, you can come to a more informed, well-thought-out decision.

In addition to the information and methodology contained in the chapters of this book, there are a number of tools in the appendix of this book and on the IACT website that will help lead you through decision-making exercises. These tools will force you to make connections and develop out-of-the-box thinking skills. I encourage you to take time to explore some of these to help improve your critical thinking.

In the next chapter, we'll discuss how to go through this process in a group, also known as team outsmarting VUCA. In some ways, this is easier, but it does require a somewhat different skill set than solo outsmarting VUCA.

TAKEAWAYS

1. Decide where and how you could create a distraction-free environment.

2. Think about individuals in your past that you can draw on for the various roles in this chapter. How could you mirror their views of the world for this exercise? Alternately, define for yourself how you believe each of these roles views the world:

    a. Who is very analytical (the Detective)?

    b. Who wears their heart on their sleeve (the Gut Check)?

c. Who is always very upbeat (the Optimist)?

d. Who is a pessimist (the Naysayer)?

e. Who has a lot of great ideas (the Creative)?

f. Who knows how to get things done (the Organizer)?

Visit the Institute for the Advancement of Critical Thinking, www.theiact.org, for more exercises to help you conduct solo VUCA thinking.

CHAPTER 5

TOOLS FOR GROUPS/TEAMS TO IMPROVE YOUR COLLECTIVE ABILITY TO OUTSMART VUCA

There's been a lot of research done on individual critical thinking: how to get better in your own thinking processes, recognize your own assumptions, evaluate your own arguments, and look at the conclusions you're drawing. Through the process I mentioned in the last chapter—playing roles, asking questions, phoning a friend, etc.—you're able to improve your own ability to outsmart VUCA. But in the workplace, especially in our Western culture, we value working in a team to put together a good argument, to sway, to influence, to persuade, to get things done.

Because we so value persuasion and influence, we tend to gloss over some of the faults in our own thinking. We tend to argue like an attorney—and an attorney's argument isn't meant to be balanced. She is either defending or prosecuting. She's supposed to argue in a certain way.

Similarly, in corporate America, we think we need to argue in a certain way in order to persuade our boss, senior management, or the customer. Again, it's all about persuasion and influence. Left unchecked and unbalanced, that mind-set is the enemy of outsmarting VUCA. It flies in the face of the type of thinking required to succeed in this rapidly changing VUCA environment.

Before you consider me brainwashed, let me go over a few limitations of the thinking required to outsmart VUCA. Alas, it is not the panacea for all that ails us.

The thinking that enables us to outsmart VUCA is especially useful in making nuanced or complex decisions, where it's key that you look at all the data and view the situation from every angle in an effort to evaluate all potential solutions and arrive at the best decision. It's not all that useful where there's a right and a wrong answer, because that's just a matter of discovery. It's also not all that useful for matters of opinion. For example, "What's your favorite food?" That's not really a decision; ten people are going to have ten different answers, and each one is equally valid. It's also not useful for factual questions that you can research—for example, how many million miles is it to the sun? That's a factual question that has a right answer. That doesn't qualify as a VUCA environment.

But where there's a best answer along with a number of other good answers, that's where this type of thinking—critical thinking—really adds value. That's where these tools, at a group level, come in.

Outsmarting VUCA in groups or teams involves similar concepts and processes employed by individuals, which I shared in the previous chapter. There are a couple of different ways this team outsmarting VUCA works best: One is a more linear process, where everyone on the team plays a different role at the same time, like in a meeting or at a brainstorming session. The other is where everyone on the team plays the same role at the same time, together moving through the sequence of roles in a group setting. Each of these processes has value, and I'll explain when it's appropriate to use one over the other.

POKING THE LION

One of the biggest challenges with practicing the team outsmarting VUCA process in corporate America arises when hierarchy is involved. That often means the boss will weigh in first and then open discussion up to the floor. "Here's what I think we ought to do, but I'm interested in hearing your opinion," he'll say. As soon as his opinion is introduced, the drive is toward a preferred solution—that being the one "suggested" by the boss. Even if the boss states his idea as an opinion, it's commonly taken as marching orders. In the interest of self-preservation and aligning with the person in charge, we find ourselves saying, "That's a brilliant idea," and now that becomes the idea to follow; we check our critical thinking at the door and just go along under the often-false assumption that to differ from the boss is career limiting.

Oftentimes, the boss is unaware of what's happening. He may even tout that he values everyone's perspective and encourages creativity and innovation, but when he asks for opinions, no one shares any that may be perceived as differing from his.

The problem largely stems from how we're set up in corporate America, in organizations. When there's a hierarchy, no one wants to poke the lion. Instead, we hold our tongue, and the lion—or the boss—doesn't recognize that's what we're doing. By remaining silent or going along with the boss, we live to fight another day.

As a result, the final decision is compromised. Opinions, gut reactions, data, etc., whether valid or invalid, are left off the table in favor of the first idea thrown out by the person with influence (who, by the way, doesn't necessarily have to be the person with the most positional authority).

. . . .

"BUT I REALLY DO
WANT YOUR INPUT"

It can be very difficult for a team to get the message that the leader really does want input.

I worked with a small, $70-million-a-year company where the management style of the founder/CEO was very dictatorial. Even though he didn't describe it that way, the entire executive team described it that way, largely because every time someone offered up an idea, the leader would directly and aggressively push back on the person giving the input.

This difference of opinion was largely based on a misunderstanding of meaning. While the CEO might say, "No, that's not the right way to look at it, this is the right way," what he really meant was, "This is my opinion of the right way to look at it, and I think I have some good reasons for that. But I'd love to hear your thoughts." This is what he meant, but that message certainly wasn't being perceived by his team.

So he was frustrated by the input he was getting from his team; he thought he didn't have the right team together, because they weren't coming up with any good ideas. But the truth was that they felt like he was a my-way-

or-the-highway leader and that offering up any idea other than his may be career limiting.

To resolve the issue, he and I worked together to change the team's perception of his openness to other ideas. We crafted a strategy where, during a typical brainstorming session, he strategically and deliberately introduced an idea that was pretty clearly not in the best interest of the company and then asked the team for their input.

Since the idea was clearly not the best idea, hesitantly, one by one, the members of the team very cautiously offered their reservations, and as part of the strategy the leader acknowledged the team members: "What I'm hearing is that you guys actually think we should go a different way instead. Do you have a different idea? I'd like to hear some alternatives."

At long last, with great fear and trepidation, one member offered an idea that was much more closely aligned with the best interests of the company. The leader verbally and non-verbally reinforced the quality of the idea and his gratitude for the team member offering it. Gradually, behaviors started to change. Ultimately, the leader convinced the team members that they had changed his mind, and the whole tenor of the room changed.

Deliberately changing a culture takes time, and it begins by getting to the root of what's

> causing that culture to exist in the first place. Treat the cause, not the symptom.

· ·

But anyone, even the lion, can make a mistake. The market may shift, new technology may disrupt, or—and this is one of the main targets of team outsmarting VUCA—the influencer may make an assumption that he is not even aware of.

When team harmony is overemphasized, it significantly hampers our ability to outsmart VUCA. Think about the nomenclature. We call ourselves "teams." If we're on a team, we're going to fight with another team. We're certainly not supposed to fight internally; that's the sign of a dysfunctional team. If my teammate says something that I disagree with, well, I don't want to fight with my own team. Instead, let's all focus on the other team and beat them.

The key is to introduce discord into a team in a safe way, in a way that allows the pros and cons to be let out in a safe environment that builds teamwork and doesn't erode the team structure. Although this sounds counterintuitive, it is possible.

Conflict is not a bad thing if it's productive, if it is done in the right way. Productive conflict allows multiple voices to be heard behind closed doors (then, when the door opens, there is a unified voice of the team to the outside world). If there's only one voice heard behind closed doors, then the thinking required to outsmart VUCA is probably not taking place—it's highly unlikely that a lone genius has more knowledge than the collective knowledge of an entire team, assuming that the team has a healthy dose of variety. That's the point of having a diverse group involved in making decisions. Without actively leveraging that diversity, you're left with only the complexity and the negatives of the team structure without any of the positives, which include the frank and honest interactions and the different perspectives.

A simple example is bringing in lunch for a group. If you're hosting lunch for the internal team, you don't really need to call a team outsmarting VUCA session. But if you're going to serve international clients, it might be good to get some weigh-in; someone in the group may bring up the fact that the clients' culture prohibits them from eating beef or that someone in the client group is a strict vegan. Good information to know if you're trying to make the right impression. Even if the boss says to order pizza, you need to have an environment where someone feels comfortable pointing out possible problems with that idea without feeling that his or her job is on the line.

Again, done collaboratively behind closed doors, this allows the team to present a unified front: "The team decided to serve up this menu—we hope you like it" is how the information would be presented.

Keep in mind that team outsmarting VUCA may not be ideally suited in times of emergency. If a decision has to be made immediately, that's not the time to get everybody in a room and have multiple voices. At some point, the boss has to be the boss and say, "The building is on fire. We all need to leave."

Although some of the tools and techniques that follow are similar to those for solo outsmarting VUCA, they are designed to help teams go through productive conflict in a way that leads to the best decision possible.

ROLES IN GROUPS

As I've mentioned, data is a key element in outsmarting VUCA. But the data—the facts and figures—must be gathered and evaluated unemotionally, without bias (or at least with recognized bias, since we can never truly be bias free).

When looking at the data, look for both that which can confirm the group's hypothesis and that which would disprove or challenge the group's hypothesis or the choice that it's going to make.

As I mentioned earlier, beware of confirmation bias, or only looking for data that supports the prevalent theory. For example, I can take a picture of a hundred white swans and formulate a theory that all swans are white. But to disprove my theory, all I need is a picture of one black swan. That's the data I need to look for . . . and that's also the challenge. Subconsciously, we don't really want to find that one black swan, because that would mean our theory that all swans are white is wrong.

The purpose of the team outsmarting VUCA process is to expose, identify, and correct individual errors of thinking and the most common errors in an argument.

Similar to the way an individual goes through roles in the solo process to outsmart VUCA, groups can also employ this pattern. When going through the roles, the members of the group are forced to argue in a different way. Even if you don't believe in the position of the particular role you are being asked to play, you can still play the role. In fact at that point it becomes less personal because the counter idea or argument against the prevailing theory is actually coming from the role itself, not from the individual playing the role. This helps get around some of the issues relating to existing relationships and hierarchy in teams: "Don't pick on me, I'm just playing the Naysayer" could be a response when someone objects to your comment criticizing an idea.

In the previous chapter, we talked about several roles and how the individual can employ them in outsmarting VUCA: the Detective, the Gut Check, the Naysayer, the Optimist, the Creative, and the Organizer. These are the same roles to use in the group process to outsmart VUCA.

In the group process, the number of roles expands or contracts depending on the decision the group is trying to make.

For example, you may want to add in perspectives from suppliers, customers, competitors, target demographics, and others—anyone who has an impact on, or who is impacted by, the decision that the group is making. You can easily add roles to the activity in order to ensure those voices are also present at the table. The more diversity of perspectives, the better the overall results will be—provided the group interacts with constructive conflict.

In order for this group process of outsmarting VUCA to work, it has to be a bit of an exercise, almost like a game. It needs to be high-energy and enjoyable, because that taps into different parts of the brain and reduces judgment during the activity. Think of it like an ink-jet printer. In many ink-jet printers, four different inks work together to produce a beautiful picture. But each color has to contribute in order to get there. That's the value of roles; you have to go through all of the relevant ones to get a complete picture, one that contains all the nuances of the different insights.

The process is driven by questions. If you're the Naysayer, you're the one to ask about risks, external threats, future exposure. If you're the Optimist, you'll inquire about the potential of the issue: How can you leverage the topic at hand? What's the upside for customers if this product is developed? Here is an example of a typical question that each role needs to ask and have answered:

- Detective: What data would cause us to abandon this decision?
- Gut Check: Would we be okay with our decision on the front page of the newspaper?
- Naysayer: What's the biggest risk with this decision?
- Optimist: What add-on opportunities would this allow us to pursue?

- Creative: How can we leverage some emerging technology to improve the results from this decision or to increase the likelihood of success?
- Organizer: What unresolved issues still exist that must be addressed before we move forward?

· ·

Want to know more?
Visit the Institute for the Advancement of
Critical Thinking, www.theiact.org.

· ·

APPROACHES FOR OUTSMARTING VUCA AS A TEAM: SERIES, PARALLEL, DIALOGUE

Once the roles are decided, the group goes through the outsmarting VUCA process in one of three ways—series, parallel, or dialogue.

Series Approach. With a series approach, the group as a whole looks at the situation through each of the roles, one role at a time. For example, perhaps the group starts by looking at the situation from the perspective of the Optimist. In this role, the group goes through the same set of questions at the same time and tries to answer each question based on what the Optimist might say or think. This forces everyone to think about the situation or the decision from essentially the same perspective.

The benefit of this approach is that it lends itself to alignment and commonality of vision. There tends to be less conflict with this approach, so it is useful if you have a team that is just forming and hasn't yet identified productive norms of behavior. It is also useful if you have an existing group where unproductive conflict has already been the norm.

After the group has thoroughly thought through the situation from the first perspective, or role, then it switches to the next role, maybe the Naysayer role. In this role, everyone tries to think what could possibly go wrong with a situation. Maybe someone tosses out an idea like market shifts; just like in "traditional" brainstorming, if someone else in the group responds that the idea couldn't possibly happen, that's against the rules. Everyone must stay in the ascribed role for the series approach to outsmarting VUCA to deliver the best results.

Parallel Approach. The second approach to outsmarting VUCA in a group is to do it in a parallel fashion, where individuals in a group are each assigned a particular role. This approach is not recommended for groups that are experiencing unproductive conflict; attempting to use this approach with such a group could lead to disaster, as you're merely throwing fuel on the fire that is smoldering just below the surface.

The parallel approach can be done in a couple of ways. One way is to assign a role to a person based on his or her own personal propensity toward a certain role. For example, if one of the members of the group is an engineer who's been with the company since it started, and he's the person in the company who always sees the potential problems no matter the situation, then you might assign him the role of the Naysayer. Or if you have a salesperson who's always looking at the upside of every situation, you may assign her the role of Optimist.

One of the principal drawbacks of assigning roles to people essentially based on how they are wired is that the person in the role is perceived as playing himself or herself. Sometimes, if the role is too closely aligned to the person's natural style, there's confusion about whether the role or the individual is speaking. Since this is often done in an existing group with existing relationships and varying levels of hierarchy, this approach can cause a multitude of issues. Among these is the issue I discussed earlier in the chapter, which is the perceived negative effect on the person's career if she says something that's not aligned with the boss, even if she believes she is saying it only from the perspective of a particular role.

Since the goal of role-playing is to remove the personal contribution and allow contributions from individual roles—in order to get away from the sense that it's the individual that's speaking out—sometimes it works better to assign people to roles that they are not comfortable with, that aren't aligned with their normal style.

For example, you might assign the problem-finding engineer to the Creative role. Now his role is to think outside the box, which goes against his normal style. Then when he suggests combining this item and that item for a possible solution, everyone knows it's the role that's talking, not the engineer himself.

The challenge to assigning roles that are outside normal behaviors is that it can take a little work on the part of the individual to get into the role because that's not how his or her brain is naturally wired.

The primary upside of working in one of the parallel approaches is that it tends to be faster than the series approach. Everyone contributes at the same time in their different roles. Unfortunately, if there is one very strong personality or a very good arguer in the group, he or she can tend to dominate the conversation at the expense of the other roles. This issue is eliminated when using the series approach because everyone participates at the same time in a given role.

Dialogue Approach. A third way of outsmarting VUCA in a group is with the dialogue approach. In this approach, the person who needs to make the decision talks one-on-one with different people outside of a group setting and asks those people to play different roles. So if I'm the person needing to make a decision, I reach out to different people and ask them to take specific roles. Then I ask each of those people what questions they have of me while they are in that role. For example, I may ask one person to be in the Naysayer role and then ask them to pose a series of relevant questions to me while in that role.

This approach takes a little longer, since it is done in a sequential fashion, but it tends to draw out the team members who may be a bit hesitant about the concept of taking on a role ("acting" or "pretending") in front of their peers. And a positive by-product is that it also serves to strengthen the relationships between the boss and the team members. Everyone feels listened to and believes they have had input into the decision being made. This often leads to higher levels of engagement and improved morale on the team.

WHICH APPROACH TO USE?

Whichever approach you choose, the process is again driven by questions. The series approach goes through the questions for each role in a group setting and attempts to answer them collectively. With the parallel approach, each role has a voice asking questions from their perspective and answering questions from the other roles essentially at the same time. Using the dialogue approach, each role has one-on-one time with the person trying to make the decision, asking questions from the role they were asked to assume.

The key is to exhaust all the questions with each role, whether it's as a group tackling the questions for one role at a time, or each person in the group assuming a specific role, or the decision maker approaching each role one at a time. This takes discipline, since "I don't know" is not an acceptable (final) answer.

Which approach you take really depends on the importance of the decision and the criticality of speed in the process.

If this is a decision that could make or break the company, the series approach is arguably the best choice because it's the best guarantee that you won't miss anything. It takes longer, but it tends to be much more thorough in its analysis of all the issues, the information, and the data from every perspective.

If the risk associated with the decision or importance of the decision is relatively low—in other words, you just need to make a quick decision—then the parallel approach will probably suffice. If you miss one or two minor ideas using this approach for a less-crucial decision, then it's not the end of the world, because the impact is fairly low. The parallel approach is much faster but may not be quite as thorough. It's more of a "ready, fire, aim" approach than "ready, aim, fire," while the series approach could be described as "ready, aim, aim, aim, okay now fire."

GETTING CONSENSUS

Once you've gathered all the input from the various roles, then it's time to work toward consensus.

A key part of this process is to work with each role to determine the first "off-ramp" from each point of view. For example, given the proposed resolution to the issue at hand, ask the Naysayer for the first indication of what could go wrong. In other words, on the road to resolving the issue, where would the Naysayer see the first indication that the plan was going to go awry? Where is the first "off-ramp" on that road?

Let's say you're putting together a three-year strategy. Where in the first month or two could you gather information that would allow you to reevaluate the group's decision and decide if you were still on the right road? How soon can you know, and what data can you look at, to find out as quickly as possible that this was not the best approach? How fast can you fail?

At the first indication that the project may derail, bring the group back to the table and evaluate using the roles again, incorporating the new data and the most relevant information currently available.

Let me share with you a real-world example of this. In my aerospace days when I worked with the Titan IV missile, we would launch from Cape Canaveral. Now, launches would often be delayed for one reason or another, so we got to explore the Florida area. During one memorable trip, we took a bit of a wrong turn and ended up on Florida's Turnpike, Route 91. (This was before smartphones with built-in global positioning systems.) Once you got on that turnpike, you were on it; there were no off-ramps between Exit 193 (Yeehaw Junction) and Exit 242 (Kissimmee/St. Cloud), a stretch of almost fifty miles. We quickly realized that we were going in the wrong direction, but there was nothing we could do until we got to Exit 242; we had to travel that entire distance to Exit 242 knowing that we had made a wrong turn. That's failing slowly. (In fairness to Florida's Turnpike, there are periodic places along the road to make effective U-turns, but in California, where I'm from, those are primarily reserved for law enforcement vehicles only, so we drove right past them.)

In business, you don't want to fail slowly, so you need to build in off-ramps. Ask the team what needs to be validated or invalidated. If you've decided that every swan is white based on the data you now have, where is the first off-ramp to evaluate that decision? If you come back in three weeks and someone has found a picture of a black swan, you'll know you haven't made the best decision, and you can adjust accordingly.

THE BEHAVIOR OF THE TEAM

The key to success with this process is for everyone to participate, and as in brainstorming, everyone must feed off each other. Unfortunately, what often happens is that someone disengages from the process. Often it's someone like the person who sees the glass half-empty but just lets the glass-half-full personalities run with the ball. But that's a key rule: everyone must participate fully and actively.

Earlier I talked about the IDEO product development firm and its process called the "Deep Dive," where the members of the group assume they know absolutely nothing about the product they're developing. Even if it's just an improvement on something that already exists, instead of modifying the product incrementally they assume they know nothing about it. They go into discovery mode and approach the product with a blank piece of paper: How is this thing used? What does this product do? What does it need to do? In the earlier example of the shopping cart, the team approached the redesign as if they had never seen shopping carts being used before. Then they observed, took notes, snapped photographs, and asked people who were using the shopping carts a variety of questions to determine what might influence the design.

When this works, the value comes from the diversity of the members on the team. The members of the team assume they have no subject-matter expertise, but they bring their own particular expertise to the table. The diversity of the way people think is absolutely essential in order to make the group process for outsmarting VUCA work. If you have the good fortune of having built (or inherited) a diverse team already, then you have a distinct advantage. If you have a more homogenous team, the importance of team members getting into the roles becomes all that more important. That's why you need scripted questions.

If you do not have diversity, you've got to create diversity, even if it's artificially created. You could also invite an outsider to the team, someone who thinks completely differently, and have him or her throw out a grenade of an idea. Maybe even invite your kids; young ones can be especially helpful because they don't know what questions not to ask. They might ask, "Why is it square?" "Because it's always been square." "Well, why don't you do it in more of a smushy kind of shape, like an amoeba?" Kids tend to question things that adults just accept as nonnegotiable facts.

The beauty of role-playing in the group process is that the discussion can get pretty lively. That's okay because the roles are doing the talking, not the members of the team themselves. Again, the goal is to keep the roles on task; if someone brings up a pessimistic challenge while the group is in the Optimist role (using the series approach), then she's inappropriately switching roles and the group must let her know that she needs to get back on track.

One of the main purposes of using the roles is to make the entire questioning process nondefensive. If one role offers a contradictory question or statement to another role, then it should be viewed as coming from the role, not from the team member. This allows the team member to say, "It's not me saying that, boss, it's the role saying it. I'm not saying it's a stupid idea, I'm just playing the role of the Naysayer." If done correctly, the roles remove the issue of hierarchy (real or perceived) and provide a safe forum where people can say things under the auspices of a role that they perhaps would feel less comfortable saying as themselves.

THE MIND-SET OF THE COMPANY LEADER

In some environments, for example, SpaceX, a firm that designs, manufactures, and launches rockets and spacecraft, challenging one another in roles—asking difficult questions, getting difficult answers—is the norm. In working with the folks there,

I've found that the culture seems to value constructive conflict. Managers who try to motivate and influence others based on hierarchy and positional authority are not a particularly good fit in that culture.

But smaller companies often have a culture based on hierarchy; the founder is also the CEO, and whatever the founder says, goes. In this situation, you're not starting the role-playing from a blank piece of paper, you're starting from a well-defined pattern of behavior in the organization. In an organization like this, the CEO may first need to be convinced that he is not getting the best answer possible; in truth, he's only getting his own answer because people are going along with him even if they don't believe his idea is best. As I mentioned earlier, no one wants to "poke the lion."

In a case like this, it's important for the boss/owner/CEO to communicate to the team that he may not have the best idea, that his voice is only one of many. He needs to inform the team that the role-playing forum is about surfacing good ideas, that it's a place where they can talk honestly without fear of repercussion, that it's about outsmarting VUCA.

Sometimes the hierarchy is so ingrained in the culture that even an introduction like that from the boss doesn't promote real role-playing. The boss may tell the team, "I'm open, please challenge me," but the perception is still skepticism—remember what happened to the last guy who did that? In that case, I recommend that the boss step aside from the process and allow another facilitator to lead the group process.

Creating a culture that encourages input doesn't happen overnight. People who offer an opinion different than the boss's must be rewarded for it—even disproportionately rewarded, I would argue, at least for a time, in order to reinforce that behavior throughout the organization. Instead of negating someone's opinion with statements like, "You know, I don't think that's the right idea," the boss needs to use affirming statements like "Interesting, tell me more" or "That wasn't what I initially thought, but brilliant idea. What do the rest of you think about that?"

If you're an employee reading this book and you see your manager making a grave error in the way he makes decisions but you don't know how to approach him, hand him this book (or just anonymously leave a copy on his desk!). It will explain to him not only the value in leveraging diversity of opinions and perspectives to outsmart VUCA but also the process for going through it. It will give him a road map to follow in leading the group, the team, or even the company to making the best decisions. Better yet, have him check out the Institute for the Advancement of Critical Thinking at www.theiact.org. There he can learn a lot more about outsmarting VUCA.

If you've got a great relationship with your manager, have a one-on-one with him. Maybe suggest getting the team together to go through this group role-playing process to outsmart VUCA.

If you don't have a good relationship, but you think the boss is a reasonable person, one option may be to lead with questions. (Are you seeing a pattern here?) Ask him, "I'm assuming your perspective is right, boss, but what are the risks if you're not entirely correct?" Think about the situation from a roles perspective. Identify why the idea is not the best. Is it because the boss is missing one of the risks? Then step into the Naysayer role. Is your boss about to miss an upside opportunity? Then take the role of the Optimist, and ask him questions like "What opportunities might we be missing if we choose to abandon this product?"

The goal is to ask questions to get him to discover for himself what he's missing. Don't go through the process sequentially; your boss is already thinking in a particular way. For example, if you've got a boss who is optimistic and never sees the negative and what you need to have him discover is the negative impact of his idea, then you've got to assume that Naysayer role and ask him the questions to get him to tap into that perspective within himself.

The team outsmarting VUCA process is similar to having four people standing around a house and describing it on a conference call, but each person sees a different side: one sees a door, one sees a balcony, etc. The key is to get everyone aligned; everyone looks at the front of the house and sees the door, then everyone looks at the back and sees the balcony, and so on. Ideally, by raising questions, you'll provide insight that the boss didn't have—maybe he didn't notice that the house had a balcony. Then you can help him come to a different decision.

The benefit of approaching the boss in this manner is that you don't go in trying to prove him wrong—instead, you go in trying to discover why he was right and in the process expose him to a perspective that he hasn't considered. Intention is critical for this to work. (One caveat: Before approaching the boss, consider that maybe he has walked all the way around the house, and it's you who are only looking at one side of it.)

When I first started experimenting with this approach, I found it immensely helpful to assume I was conversing with Albert Einstein about the theory of relativity. The theory doesn't make sense to me, but I'm probably safe in assuming that Albert is a bit brighter than me. So I might say, "Okay, here's what I see, Dr. Einstein. Your theory says that moving clocks run more slowly, but this doesn't make sense to me. I move my watch back and forth quickly and it doesn't appear to run any slower. So please help me understand what I'm missing." It would be egotistical and arrogant to try to prove to Albert Einstein that he's wrong about the theory of relativity. It's a similar rationale with a boss. The best approach is to assume your boss is legitimately right and then to ask questions to understand what you're missing in order to figure out why he's right. It's a totally different intent, and trying to prove him wrong can be rather career limiting.

Whatever your intent, if your boss shuts you down and says he's absolutely certain that he's right, then the dialogue is over. At that point, there's not much you can do, and you just need to walk away. Choose carefully what hill on which you wish to die.

Earlier I talked about the gift store I worked at that sold only high-end stuffed animals and was incredibly successful in a mall in the Santa Barbara area. But then the owner decided to expand into the Bakersfield area, which ultimately led to the company's closure. As one of his assistant managers, I had done a little market research before the expansion.

While the existing mall location boomed during the year-end holiday season, in the summertime there was very little business at the store. However, there was a nearby beach with a pier over the ocean called Stearn's Wharf where a gift shop happened to be going out of business at the same time we were looking to expand. It was a small space, but Stearn's Wharf was a very busy tourist attraction during the summer months and rather slow in the winter. I thought it would perfectly balance the business at the mall, and I told the owner so. (I even wanted to carry more touristy merchandise and call the store "Santa Bar-bear-a.")

Alas, I was overruled. The owner chose instead to expand to Bakersfield because it was the fastest-growing city in California at the time and, well, I've told you the rest of the story. The point is that I had the choice to push the conversation further in order to expose the faulty logic or to walk away.

When people are not open to questioning their own assumptions, there's not much you can do to open someone else's mind. It can be especially tough for business owners and entrepreneurs. They see themselves as bold explorers, conquering the world: "I'm not wrong. I'm going to take a gamble, and I'm going to make it."

According to an interview with the BBC, Elon Musk was convinced that "SpaceX maybe had a 10 percent chance at success," but he didn't put his head in the sand. He looked for all those early signs that it wasn't going to work, and he reached a point where he knew that the next launch determined the company's success or failure. He kept pushing, making progress, taking the company to the next level, and demanding constructive conflict on a daily basis. Thankfully, that pivotal launch was a success. That's the sign of a good leader—someone who's open to questioning their own assumptions, getting outside data and opinions, and recognizing there's a chance they made the wrong call.

PROCESS BEST PRACTICES

There's no one right or wrong way of going through the team outsmarting VUCA process. The key is flexibility. There are, however, some best practices.

If you're using the series process, you should have a facilitator for the meeting, preferably not the boss. And the facilitator should be knowledgeable and skilled in the tools and processes associated with team outsmarting VUCA as outlined in this book.

If you have a big group, then you may need to break it into smaller groups. An ideal size is between four and six people (for the series process) because then everybody has a voice. In groups larger than this, people tend to tune out and check their smartphones.

As you step through the series process, gather the different ideas and post them on a wall. Then transition to the next role and continue to move sequentially through the different roles.

While it can be viewed as a role-playing game, it needs to be orderly and focused. With the series approach, don't hop back and forth between the roles, and don't let anyone deviate from the current role until everyone goes together.

The rules are a little different for the parallel approach. Each individual must adhere to their role, but then the process can be flexible. You can do one round where everyone represents their role at the same time; however, this can be very chaotic, and it also doesn't guarantee that everybody's voice is equally heard. This is especially true if you've got someone who is not a verbal processor; they may tune out, go to their happy place, and not contribute. Then the process breaks down. But if it's not a critical decision, an 80 percent solution may still work.

If you need a more thorough solution, either process in series or use the parallel approach but rotate the roles. By rotating the roles, I mean maybe do a second or even third round where everyone shifts one role to the right. This can help you get a more thorough, well-vetted decision without going through the entire series process . . . sort of a hybrid approach.

CONCLUSION

The biggest challenge in the group process for outsmarting VUCA arises when the company leader fears or resists conflict or is too hierarchical. He may respect his people for what they know, but he believes he should be in the lead and that conflict is a sign of disrespect or dysfunction in the team. Like Henry Ford, who was quoted as saying, "Why does every pair of hands have to come with a brain attached?" Ford was a company leader who did not seem to want the opinions of the people who were working for him. He was the founder of the company, and he knew the best approach . . . just ask him!

That's where the group process is most vulnerable, and that's one of the biggest risks to any organization. With the amount of volatility, uncertainty, complexity, and ambiguity that we're in right now and that is facing us in the near future, leaders simply cannot do things the way they've been doing them for the past five years and expect to succeed in the next five years. You, as a leader, have got to think differently.

Effectively leveraging the diversity of opinion that exists on your team or in your organization is what's going to lead you to the right decision. The odds are stacked against a lone genius being right every single time in this VUCA environment. You've got to give power to the team, you've got to leverage the diversity of the team. You've got to allow for enlightened trial and error. You've got to say, "Well, let's try this and see if it works," and then learn like crazy. As Google says, "Fail fast!"

As a leader, if you don't want to create an environment that fosters a narrow and dysfunctional way of thinking, if every day has to be your way or no way, you're facing the very real risk of driving your company into a wall. You may be selling the best buggy whips ever produced, but you're going to get run over by the car.

Playing these roles communicates the message that it's okay to poke holes in an idea. Consider this: if the boss takes the role of Naysayer, then it's his responsibility to argue against himself because now he has to consider what could possibly go wrong with his own idea.

Outsmarting VUCA with this group process is one way to paint the complete picture of the situation, to get every valuable perspective in the room in a way that is safe and that doesn't create the perception in the minds of the participants that differing from the leader may end up being career limiting.

TAKEAWAYS

1. Think about which group approach to outsmarting VUCA will work best in your organization: series, parallel, dialogue?

2. If you're a CEO reading this book, ask yourself: Is VUCA impacting my organization? And am I inadvertently stifling dissension in my team? How can I know for sure?

3. If you're an employee reading this book, how could you use these processes to begin to sway your organization's leader to a different way of thinking?

Visit the Institute for the Advancement of Critical Thinking, www.theiact.org, for more group exercises for outsmarting VUCA.

CHAPTER 6

ACTION PLAN / GAUGING RESULTS

Your existing patterns of thinking took years to evolve and develop—don't expect those patterns to change overnight. You've got to have the desire to change, the willingness to change, and the ability to change. I hope this book has helped with the desire and the ability. Now you've got to have the willingness.

Having read this book, you should now have the knowledge to recognize and be able to identify the fallacies and errors in reasoning that are part of our everyday lives.

Behavior changes take time. Pattern changes take time. It's a journey, and the journey itself is the process. You'll never be able to completely and perpetually outsmart VUCA. That's not the goal. The goal is to improve individual and group thinking one step at a time. The goal is to start chipping away at the most dysfunctional patterns in our own thinking and in our team thinking in order to begin the process of thinking more effectively in this volatile, uncertain, complex, and ambiguous world.

The key is to identify that most valuable first step. The step that will produce the most direct result in your current situation may be personal or group level. To identify that, figure out what actions you can take to make progress, and then put a plan in place to actually take that step.

To help you as you embark on the journey to become a better thinker, I've developed an action plan that's available online at the Institute for the Advancement of Critical Thinking, www. theiact.org. This action plan contains instructions for how best to make changes to get better at outsmarting VUCA, both individually and in a group environment. It contains information about objectives, a time frame, and tips on how to work with an accountability partner to help you achieve your objectives.

On the individual level, you'll find space in the action plan for the goals and the objectives: What do you want to improve or get better at? It might be a specific fallacy that you've recognized in your own thinking, or it might be making a decision and ensuring that you are thinking as effectively as possible and using unbiased information to come to the best decision possible.

The individual action plan will also help you set some short- and long-term goals that will help you improve your thinking skills. It also includes information to help you work as an individual in a group setting.

I hope you'll use this to recognize your own biases and begin to apply some of these critical-thinking skills.

COMPONENTS OF THE PLAN

When setting goals as part of critical thinking, they should be SMART—specific, measurable, aligned, realistic, and as time-bound as possible. (Yes, I recognize this is a different SMART acronym from Peter Drucker, but bear with me; there's a reason for the difference.)

With individual and group thinking, the level of specificity and the immediacy of the steps are going to vary depending on whether it's a short-term or long-term goal. Short-term goals are for the issues you're facing right now, such as a decision you need to make this week. Maybe you're having a meeting on strategy or expansion plans; this is an opportunity for an immediate, short-term application of the knowledge and skills. The outcome of the activity should be measurable, perhaps with a checklist indicating whether the skills were applied correctly.

The long-term goals are more developmental. These are a little bit like going on a diet; the immediate action I'm going to take is to get rid of all my junk food in my pantry. In the longer term, I'm going to a gym and starting an exercise regime. In 180 days, my goal is to have lost twenty pounds and have run a half marathon.

You also need to have a plan for accountability. A number of studies have found that having an accountability partner is the key to long-term success. In Alcoholics Anonymous, for example, eliminating the accountability partner during recovery resulted in a dramatic drop in the success rate of the entire program.

In business, you've got to have someone who is not afraid to challenge you, who hopefully has already traveled the path that you are traveling, and who is either good at outsmarting VUCA or is at a higher level of management, where they can almost be a mentor to you.

In other words, it shouldn't be someone who reports to you. That just makes for a very awkward relationship when it comes to challenging you and holding you accountable. It should also be somebody with whom you have frequent contact and with whom you have an honesty commitment. It should be someone who is willing and able to challenge you without fear of repercussions.

The hesitancy that I find most often with my executive coaching clients when looking for an accountability partner is their own; they worry about imposing on someone else. Instead, I've found that the accountability partner is usually flattered or honored to take on the role. So you must have the courage to take that step. The worst thing that might happen is you might have to go with a second choice.

MEASURING BEHAVIORAL CHANGE

How do you measure improvement in outsmarting VUCA? The best way is to measure the outcomes.

Measuring is also about looking for the off-ramps, looking for those decision points along the way. Make the best decision possible at the time with the information that you have, and then constantly reevaluate the decision.

As you progress, you need to ask questions such as: Has any new information come to light that impacts the situation or this decision? Has a stakeholder recently come on the scene that I should have identified earlier that has now changed the level of available information that I've got? Is my finger on the pulse of all the industry surveys that could possibly weigh into this decision? Is there someone in my sphere who thinks differently than me that I'm avoiding interacting with but who could actually add value to this discussion?

What information specifically would affect my analysis or would affect my conclusion? And then how do I go about finding that information or ensuring that I'm not missing relevant information?

How do I validate that my conclusion is the best one possible? For example, if you made a decision that is directly tied to gaining market share and you don't gain market share, is that an indication that you made a wrong decision? Maybe, but it could also indicate a shift in the marketplace that you didn't adjust to, that you didn't see coming.

It's a little bit like predicting the stock market or the economic recovery. Ideally, you would find those leading indicators, and they would precede a good decision. Unfortunately, as with the stock market, it's often the lagging indicators that give us a reading. And by then, it's too late to be proactive.

That's why we build in off-ramps to help us adjust as we go along. We have to build in not only the metrics around the lagging indicators (and hopefully also the leading indicators) but also the decisions about what to do when the indicators are different than what we expected based on the decision that we made.

If you are an individual measuring your results, it's a matter of self-reflection. Are you thinking about your thinking? Can you answer that honestly? Have you gone through and recognized that you are not making any of the errors in reasoning? That may be the best measure on a short-term basis.

Another measure would be with the accountability partner. Does he or she see errors in your thinking? Are you actively seeking out people who have a different opinion or a different perspective?

When you're evaluating your results, go back through the decision and ask yourself if you're applying any of the common patterns of weak arguments. Have you asked the questions honestly and taken the time to answer them? Then ask yourself which questions you skipped over or answered with one or two words because they made you uncomfortable. Which questions didn't you think applied? Did you avoid answering any questions because they led to a different conclusion that you didn't like? Pay particular attention to those fallacies that you know you are prone to. Do you tend to be guilty of confirmation bias? If so, you might only be looking for data that supports your existing view. What data would counteract or contradict the decision that you made? What's an early indicator that you made the wrong decision or that you may need to adjust the decision that you made?

CONCLUSION

If anywhere in your world you operate in a VUCA environment—a place that is volatile, uncertain, complex, and ambiguous—then you absolutely need to strengthen your critical-thinking skills. Moving forward in a global environment, the skills required to outsmart VUCA—identifying your own assumptions, evaluating your own arguments and the arguments of others, and coming to conclusions in the most expedient and thorough way possible—will lead to a competitive advantage both individually as well as organizationally.

For the company leader, this type of thinking is crucial for adjusting, steering, and changing your organization and your strategy in a way that maximizes success, whether that's deemed to be profitability, market share, impact, or or some other metric. Whatever measurement you are targeting as an organization, these thinking skills as a leader are key enablers of that success. What you don't want to do is make a wrong decision and not realize it until it's too late to make any adjustments.

You need your team to be better at outsmarting VUCA as well. To do that, you need to drive these skills throughout your organization. As the leader, you've got to not only demonstrate your commitment to outsmarting VUCA but also reward the behaviors as you see them throughout your organization. When you see someone who has made a decision and has reasoned through it using some of the skills and techniques in this book, by calling out and rewarding that behavior you will drive these skills through your entire organization.

The lone genius is not a surefire recipe for success anymore. You've got to have distributed decision making, empowered employees, and engaged teams. You've got to be able to assign the authority and the responsibility as low as possible in any organization. When you do that, you must ensure they've got the skills to be able to make the best decision possible. And that's where these skills to outsmart VUCA come in.

Think of this as a commitment. It's a new habit. It's unlearning an existing behavioral pattern and learning a new one, replacing it with a new way of thinking. It doesn't happen overnight and under stress, and the temptation will be to fall right back into the old way of doing things.

If you are in a high-stress environment, go easy on yourself. When you're first starting out, try to choose a situation in which you are not under incredible time pressure or at an incredibly high risk. Essentially, practice riding the bike with training wheels first. Practice these skills, get good at them, and then start applying them in high-stress environments, if at all possible. Otherwise, studies show over and over that you will have a much higher probability of falling right back into old patterns because that's what you are comfortable with, that's what you are familiar with, that's how you know how to make decisions.

Once you get good at this, I can tell you that you will do it almost absentmindedly. It will become part of your modus operandi, the way you operate. That's when you and your organization really get the value out of thinking in a way to outsmart VUCA.

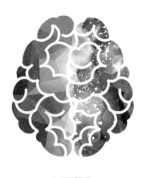

APPENDIX

QUESTION CONSTRUCTS TO OUTSMART VUCA

Throughout this book, it has been emphasized that one of the core skills required to Outsmart VUCA is asking the right question(s) rather than just trying to find the "right" answers. Fortunately, this is a skill that can be acquired, improved, and practiced. According to Bloom's Revised Taxonomy of Cognitive Processes, there are six levels of cognition that questions can target. For outsmarting VUCA, all six levels are valuable and should be emphasized varyingly, depending on the context of the situation. The six levels are:

Level 1: Knowledge—the ability to identify and recall facts, opinions, and concepts.

Level 2: Comprehension—the ability to organize and interpret information in one's own words.

Level 3: Application—the ability to use and apply what is learned to a new situation.

Level 4: Analysis—the ability to determine internal relationships and separate a whole into component parts.

Level 5: Evaluation—the ability to make judgments, opinions, or decisions using criteria and standards.

Level 6: Creation/Synthesis—the ability to put facts together into a coherent whole, or, creatively achieve a new understanding by linking facts together.

So what type of questions address each of these levels? While there are many more examples of specific questions on the Institute for the Advancement of Critical Thinking's website, www.theiact.org, here are some basic constructs that will enable you to form your own questions that address each level specifically.

LEVEL 1: KNOWLEDGE

These questions really address the recall of previously learned information by recalling facts, definitions, basic concepts, and answers already generated. These often include four of the five Ws and the H (who, what, where, when, and how). In addition to these, other typical words used in these questions are: cite; define; describe; fill in the blank; find; list; identify; label; locate; match; name; recall; select; spell; state; tell; write.

Example question constructs:

- What is _____?

- When did _____ happen?

- How would you explain _____?

- Where did _____ happen?

- How would you describe _____?

- How did _____ happen?

- Can you recall _____?

- Who was _____?

- Can you list three _____?

LEVEL 2: COMPREHENSION

These questions focus on understanding of facts and ideas by organizing, comparing, translating, interpreting, describing, stating main ideas, etc. Typical words used in Level 2 questions are: associate; conclude; convert; describe; discuss; estimate; explain; generalize; interpret; note; paraphrase; put in order; restate in your own words; rewrite; summarize.

Example question constructs:

- How would you compare/contrast _____?

- In your own words, how would you explain _____?

- What ideas and/or facts demonstrate _____?

- What evidence is there that _____?

- What is the main idea of _____?

- Can you provide an example of _____?

- What differences exist between _____?

- How would you rephrase _____?

- What data supports _____ and what data contradicts _____?

LEVEL 3: APPLICATION

These questions focus on problem solving by applying acquired knowledge, facts, models, tools, techniques, and rules in a different way. Typical words used in Level 3 questions are: apply; change; compute; conclude; construct; demonstrate; determine; draw; experiment; find out; give an example of; illustrate; interpret; make; modify; practice; show; solve; use; utilize.

Example question constructs:

- What other examples can you find to _____?

- How would you demonstrate your understanding of _____?

- What approach would you suggest to _____?

- What might have happened if _____?

- How is _____ an example of _____?

- Why is _____ related to _____?

- Why is _____ significant?

- Do you know of another instance where _____?

- Could this have happened in _____?

- What could result if _____?

- How can you organize _____ to show _____?

LEVEL 4: ANALYSIS

These questions examine and decompose information into parts by identifying motives/causes, making inferences, discovering evidence to support generalizations, etc. Typical words used in Level 4 questions are: analyze; appraise; categorize; classify; compare; contrast; determine the factors; diagram; differentiate; dissect; distinguish; divide; examine; explain; identify; infer; scrutinize; separate; specify.

- What inference can you make from _____?

- How would you classify _____?

- How would you break _____ apart?

- What are the various elements of _____?

- Is there a "Black Swan" we can find that would contradict our generalization that _____?

- What would be the consequences of _____?

- What are the parts or features of _____?

- What is similar to _____?

- What is different than _____?

- What evidence can you present for _____?

- How is _____ related to _____?

- What conclusions can you draw?

- What is the relationship between _____ and _____?

- Is there a distinction between _____ and _____?

- What ideas justify _____?

- What is the function of _____?

LEVEL 5: EVALUATION

These questions are designed to present ideas and defend opinions by making judgments about information, validity of ideas, quality of work based on a known set of criteria, etc. Typical words used in Level 5 questions are: appraise; argue; assess; calculate; choose; compare; conclude; convince; critique; decide; defend; estimate; evaluate; gauge; give your opinion; judge; justify; measure; prioritize; rank; rate; recommend; select; support; value; verify; weigh.

- How would you compare _____ and _____?

- Which do you think is better, _____ or _____?

- How would you evaluate the contribution of _____ to _____?

- What was the value/importance of _____ in _____?

- What would you have recommended if you had been
  _____?

- What criteria would you use to assess _____?

- How would you decide about _____?

- What is your opinion of _____?

- How could you disprove _____?

- Based on what you know, how can you explain
  _____?

- What information can you use to support the view
  _____?

- How would you justify _____?

LEVEL 6: CREATION/SYNTHESIS

These questions are designed to compile information together in a different way by combining elements in a new pattern or by proposing alternative solutions. Typical words used in Level 6 questions are: change; combine; compose; construct; create; design; fabricate; find an unusual way; formulate; generate; imagine; invent; predict; pretend; produce; propose; rearrange; reconstruct; reorganize; revise; suggest; suppose.

- What might have happened if _____?

- What would be an alternative interpretation of
  _____?

- How would someone from _____ interpret this information/data/situation?

- How else could we solve _____?

- What would you predict/infer from _____?

- What ideas can you add to _____?

- How would you create/design a new _____?

- What solutions would you suggest for _____?

- What would it be like if _____?

- What might happen if you combined _____ with _____?

- How can you adapt _____ to create a different _____?

- What would you predict the outcome to be if _____?

Again, each level is important when outsmarting VUCA. The lower-level questions are often easier to answer than the upper-level questions, so plan on spending additional time, especially when wrestling with Level 6 (Creation/Synthesis) questions. And you'll notice that some words or questions occur in multiple levels. This framework, or taxonomy, should be used as a guide, not a set of hard-and-fast rules. With practice, these questions will come naturally when going through the process of outsmarting VUCA, but in the beginning, you may want to take the time to write out some questions for each of the levels. You may not need all of them, and you certainly may add questions during the process, but the prework will enable you to keep the process going and gives you the best chance of producing valuable results in your efforts to outsmart VUCA.

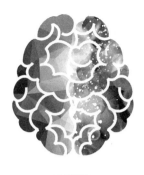

ABOUT

THE INSTITUTE FOR
THE ADVANCEMENT OF
CRITICAL THINKING

The Institute for the Advancement of Critical Thinking (IACT) is dedicated to enabling people across the globe to become better thinkers. Our belief is that volatility, uncertainty, complexity, and ambiguity are the new norm and that our educational system has done a less-than-ideal job in preparing us for this new environment. We are taught to find the "right answer" on the exam, and yet in this VUCA world there is no single "right" answer, but instead there are "better" and "worse" answers. Most of us do not have the skills and the tools to operate in this amorphous environment, and yet success as an individual, as an organization, and indeed as a country and world will depend on rapidly developing these skills, learning to use these tools, and thriving in an environment that looks quite different than the one we faced just a few years ago. The Institute for the Advancement of Critical Thinking believes that by improving our thinking, we can improve the world. You can find out more information at www.theiact.org.

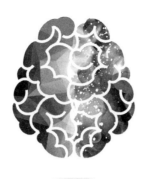

ABOUT

DON GILMAN

Don Gilman, EdD, executive director of the Institute for the Advancement of Critical Thinking, is a best-selling author, a seasoned consultant and coach to senior management, a highly sought-after speaker and trainer, and a former rocket scientist. Don has taught for various institutions, including the University of California, Los Angeles (UCLA). He has appeared on CBS, NBC, ABC, Fox, CNN, MSNBC, BBC, and other networks and has been quoted in *USA Today, The Los Angeles Times, The Orange County Register, The New York Times,* and many other national and regional newspapers and periodicals. He is also a published author in respected international journals.

Don's career spans over eight years in the aerospace industry as a rocket scientist for the Titan IV missile, including acting as mission manager for numerous secret missions. Don also spent over eight years in the automotive industry, leading the North American and European Business Unit for a privately held company that was eventually acquired by Robert Bosch GmbH.

Don has worked with over one hundred companies, including Microsoft, Google, SpaceX, and many others. Don holds a bachelor's degree (with honors) in engineering physics from Westmont College, a bachelor's degree in nuclear engineering from the University of California, Santa Barbara, a master's degree in engineering management from West Coast University and a doctorate degree in organization change from Pepperdine University.